NAIS

Journal of the NATIVE AMERICAN *and*
INDIGENOUS STUDIES ASSOCIATION

VOLUME 4.1

Spring 2017

NAIS (ISSN 2332-1261) is published two times a year by the University of Minnesota Press, 111 Third Avenue South, Suite 290, Minneapolis, MN 55401-2520. http://www.upress.umn.edu

Postmaster: Send address changes to *NAIS,* University of Minnesota Press, 111 Third Avenue South, Suite 290, Minneapolis, MN 55401-2520.

Information about manuscript submissions can be found at naisa.org, or inquiries can be sent to journal@naisa.org.

Books and other material for review should be addressed to *NAIS*, Department of American Studies, University of Kansas, Bailey Hall, Room 213, 1440 Jayhawk Boulevard, Lawrence, KS 66045-7594.

Address subscription orders, changes of address, and business correspondence (including requests for permission and advertising orders) to *NAIS,* University of Minnesota Press, 111 Third Avenue South, Suite 290, Minneapolis, MN 55401-2520.

SUBSCRIPTIONS

- **Individual subscriptions to *NAIS*** are a benefit of membership in the Native American and Indigenous Studies Association. NAISA membership is $50 annually. To become a member, visit http://naisa.org/.
- **Institutional subscriptions to *NAIS*** are $100 inside the U.S.A., $105 outside the U.S. Checks should be made payable to the University of Minnesota Press and sent to *NAIS,* University of Minnesota Press, 111 Third Avenue South, Suite 290, Minneapolis, MN 55401-2520.
- **Back issues of *NAIS*** are $25 for individuals (plus $6 shipping for the first copy, $1.25 for each additional copy inside the U.S.A.; $9.50 shipping for the first copy, $6 for each additional copy, outside the U.S.A.).
- **Digital subscriptions to *NAIS* for institutions** are available online through the JSTOR Current Scholarship Program at http://www.jstor.org/r/umnpress.

NAIS

Journal of the NATIVE AMERICAN *and* INDIGENOUS STUDIES ASSOCIATION

CONTENTS

VOLUME 4 ● ISSUE 1

Spring 2017

SAMI LAKOMÄKI, RITVA KYLLI, AND TIMO YLIMAUNU

Drinking Colonialism: Alcohol, Indigenous Status, and Native Space on Shawnee and Sámi Homelands, 1600–1850

Introduction: Alcohol and Global Indigenous History

IN THE 1830S, three very dissimilar colonial states on the opposite sides of the Atlantic launched almost simultaneous campaigns against Indigenous alcohol consumption. In less than a decade, the United States, Finland, and Sweden prohibited the production, sale, and, in some cases, drinking of intoxicating beverages on Native homelands lying within the borders claimed by the states.[1] In each country these legislative measures greatly shaped the political and legal status of Indigenous peoples and their relationship with the colonial state. The liquor laws, together with other contemporaneous legislation dealing with Indigenous rights and lands, asserted state sovereignty over Native communities and helped to construct Indigeneity as a legal and racial category that set rigid limits to Native autonomy. Moreover, they created colonial geographies in which Indigenous homelands became special legal spaces within state boundaries. Beneath these striking parallels, however, the alcohol legislation of the three states constructed Native status and space in significantly dissimilar ways. Most notably, the federal legislators in the United States recognized Native American nations as semi-sovereign entities with authority over Indigenous drinking on tribal lands, while the Finnish and Swedish lawmakers denied the aboriginal Sámi people any autonomy and instead gave state officials full power to police Native alcohol consumption everywhere.

These parallel but divergent colonial laws throw into stark relief the intimate interlinkages between alcohol, colonial state-building, and political and cultural constructions of Indigenous status and Native spaces. Scholars have long recognized alcohol as a "colonizing substance par excellence," but while earlier studies saw liquor simply as "a particularly versatile weapon in the invader's arsenal," more recent research apprehends alcohol's roles in colonialism as far more "complex and even contradictory."[2] In particular, during the past twenty years scholarly interest has expanded from alcohol's effects on Indigenous health and well-being to the politics of alcohol in colonial situations. Historians and anthropologists have demonstrated that alcohol gained diverse political meanings in variegated colonial contexts and that both Natives and newcomers mobilized it in multiple ways for a wide variety of political purposes.[3]

As these studies make clear, intoxicating beverages constituted an important meeting zone for Indigenous peoples and intruders who negotiated their relations and defined their own, as well as one another's, status by drinking, sharing, and controlling liquor. Across the colonial world, the power to drink, to regulate the drinking of others, and to assign cultural meanings to drinking constituted a crucial part in forging new relations of authority and classifying people in novel ways. Moreover, liquor consumption and control spatialized both claims to power and categories of people. By allowing or denying specific, socially constructed groups of people to drink at specific, culturally defined and demarcated places, Natives and newcomers alike imposed political meanings on the landscape, asserted authority over it, and articulated complex ideas about who belonged where and in which status.[4]

This article explores the complex connections between alcohol and the construction of Indigenous status and space in two seemingly disparate colonial contexts, eastern North America and northern Fennoscandia (the geographic area of contemporary Finland, Sweden, and Norway). It investigates how Natives and newcomers used the circulation, consumption, and control of colonial liquor to imagine and mold Indigenous sovereignty, Indigenous– state relations, and Indigenous spaces between 1600 and the 1850s, as fledgling colonial polities in both areas gradually grew into powerful territorial states. In North America, the essay zooms in on the Shawnee people and their experiences with British and, after 1776, U.S. colonialism. In Fennoscandia, the focus is on the Sámis and their encounters with the kingdom of Sweden and Finland, a province of Sweden that was annexed to the Russian empire as an autonomous grand duchy in 1809. It is important to stress from the outset that Shawnee and Sámi histories are internally immensely diverse. Both peoples have always lived in dozens of widely dispersed communities whose historical experiences have often been quite dissimilar. We concentrate on the main trends in the most thoroughly documented communities. In the Sámi case, this means emphasizing the histories of the reindeer herders in what is now northern Sweden and Finland; in the Shawnee case the focus is on the Ohio Valley groups that later relocated to Kansas. While other communities elsewhere shared many of the experiences traced here, their stories would also contain important differences.

Comparing divergent Native experiences from across the globe is vital for rethinking Indigenous histories. Native pasts have long been told in the context of the national histories of the contemporary settler states. Although this has gradually given Native peoples visibility in narratives traditionally dominated by colonists, it has also distorted Indigenous experiences by casting them as subplots in stories about the rise of today's settler societies.[5] Increasingly, scholars looking for alternative angles into Native encounters with colonialism are adopting global perspectives to challenge the state-centric histories. Colin Calloway, for instance, recently argued that American Indian history "needs to go global" and proposed that "the long histories of Native American nations" should be disentangled from "the confines of U.S. history" and recontextualized within "a global indigenous history."[6] A growing number of historians are now building precisely such a global framework through comparative analyses. Connecting and contrasting Native experiences from the Americas, Fennoscandia, Australia, New Zealand, Africa, Asia, and the Pacific, they have revealed both widespread patter and local variations in the unfolding of Native—newcomer relations. This scholarship has disrupted ofttold and universalizing stories about colonialism, highlighting the diversity of Indigenous and colonial agendas and relations, the variegated power of Native peoples in shaping colonialism, and the unpredictably intimate intersections of Native and colonial lives. On the other hand, it has helped us to better appreciate the broad structural forces shaping colonialism on Indigenous homelands, such as the rise of European racial and gender ideologies.[7]

Perhaps most important, comparative studies of Indigenous history illuminate the complex interplay between global and local forces in the making of Indigenous status, sovereignty, and space in differing political and cultural contexts. Juxtaposing diverse Native encounters with colonial alcohol sheds new light on these dialogic and contested processes. Across the world, colonial liquor became a filter through which developing European ideas about territorial sovereignty, race, nationhood, and civilization were funneled into local colonial and Indigenous settings, translated, challenged, and reshaped. Likewise, for many Native peoples alcohol provided a tool for explaining their own visions about their status and place to the colonial intruders. A comparative analysis of Shawnee and Sámi histories of alcohol consumption and control teases out how the language of liquor, and the ideas it articulated, became global and local at the same time. Simultaneously, it demonstrates how the roots of the modern cultural understandings of Indigeneity took shape at the intersections of Native and colonial ideologies, geopolitical strategies, and grassroots-level social relationships.

Investigating Sámi and Shawnee experiences with colonial liquor is complicated by the sources at our disposal, however. Well into the nineteenth century the documents recording alcohol use among both peoples were produced almost exclusively by colonial outsiders. These writers' views on drinking often differed radically from the Indigenous ones, while their attitudes toward the Natives were sometimes exceedingly negative. Together, these factors frequently led to distorted depictions of Indigenous alcohol consumption whose main purpose was to stress the alleged Otherness and savagery of the Natives. However, not all colonial reporters shared the same bias. Some, accustomed to widespread social and ritual use of liquor in their own communities, did not attach moral stigma to drinking and penned surprisingly neutral descriptions of Shawnee or Sámi alcohol consumption. As this points out, documents of Indigenous drinking require critical reading that recognizes their diversity and complexity.

In addition to such problems with available evidence, comparing Indigenous histories has its share of challenges. At the first glance, for example, Shawnee and Sámi pasts may appear too incommensurate for any meaningful comparison. When they first encountered English colonists in the seventeenth century, the Shawnees were farmers and hunters living in the Ohio Valley and organized into a multi-town confederacy. Over the next two centuries, British–American settler-colonialism pushed them violently from their homelands, a process culminating in the Indian Removal program of the United States that forced the Shawnees and thousands of their Native neighbors to reservations west of the Mississippi River in the 1830s.[8] The contemporaneous Sámis, in turn, were hunters, fishers, harvesters, and reindeer herders, spread in small and often mobile kin groups across northern and central Fennoscandia. In the seventeenth century, Scandinavian kingdoms initiated a powerful campaign to bring the Sámis and their lands under state authority, but instead of a massive settler invasion the monarchs sought to integrate the Sámis into the kingdoms as taxpaying and Christianized subjects.[9]

Not surprisingly, these histories have been narrated in radically different terms. U.S. historians have typically portrayed Shawnee history, as well as Native American history in general, as a violent story of colonial conquest in which the role of the Indigenous peoples has long been to "resist, retreat, and struggle."[10] Scandinavians, on the other hand, have traditionally stressed the "peaceful" inclusion of the Sámis into the settler states. While a growing number of scholars, many of them Sámis, today promote more critical reinterpretations of Fennoscandian history, some historians still deny that colonialism played any role in the region's past and prefer to speak of state "integration."[11] The differing North American and Fennoscandian narratives seem to be based on two opposing settler constructions of Indigenous status and place. In North America, the standard story goes, the British and their American descendants pushed the Natives *outside* the emerging colonial state as racial Others.[12] In Fennoscandia, state-builders and settlers similarly othered and racialized the Sámis, but still sought to enclose them *inside* state structures and spaces as subjects.[13]

A comparative analysis of Shawnee and Sámi histories of alcohol use challenges such simple dichotomies. From the seventeenth through the nineteenth century, colonists in both Fennoscandia and eastern North America did in fact put a lot of thought into determining whether the Native peoples they encountered belonged inside or outside the emerging settler societies and whether they should to be regarded as (potential) subjects or as something else. Settlers and state-builders in both areas participated in broader European and Atlantic conversations about territorial sovereignty, race, and nationhood that increasingly envisioned the world as a modular network of politically centralized and ethnically unified states and divided humankind into discreet national and racial entities. Drawing on these ideological currents, the colonists classified the landscape into "inside" and "outside" spaces and people into "insiders" and "outsiders."[14] Alcohol—its regulation and cultural beliefs about its use—played a central part in forging these political and spatial imaginations and in defining the place and status of Indigenous peoples within them. However, the social and physical place the colonial alcohol policies in eastern North America and northern Fennoscandia assigned to the local Native peoples was always ambiguous and contradictory. From the start, these policies located the Natives *simultaneously* inside and outside the political, legal, national, and racial spaces of the nascent settler societies.

Exploring such inconsistencies, we argue, helps scholars to apprehend how complex and confused colonial thinking about Indigenous status was on both sides of the Atlantic. Equally important, it highlights the importance of Native agency in shaping colonialism. Instead of some uniform "Indigenous" response to alcohol, Shawnees and Sámis created sharply differing politics of drinking that envisioned Native status and place in divergent ways—and their actions regarding liquor powerfully molded the forms that colonials took on their homelands.

Shared Spaces, Contested Meanings

In the seventeenth and early eighteenth century, alcohol became a key element in the trade and diplomacy between Indigenous peoples and newcomers in northern Fennoscandia and eastern North America. Initially, Natives and colonists on each side of the Atlantic used liquor to build connections and share space and resources. In both areas, alcohol took a central place in rituals of gift-giving that bound Indigenous peoples and intruders together. However, Natives and newcomers understood their relations in radically different ways, and exchanging alcohol took on great symbolic power in articulating these conflicting visions. Shawnees and Sámis alike used gift exchanges to integrate the newcomers into Native social networks, creating shared landscapes of interwoven peoples. British and Swedish colonists, in contrast, circulated alcohol to imagine and construct hierarchical imperial and state structures to which the Native peoples were to be bound in a subordinate role.

Alcohol entered Sámi and Shawnee homelands during the seventeenth century via the globalizing fur trade. Since the Middle Ages, the Sámis had sold the furs and hides of beaver, reindeer, fox, and other northern animals to Scandinavian, Finnish, and Slavic traders who channeled the goods to central Europe.[15] The Shawnees and their Native neighbors across eastern North America opened similar commercial contacts with Europeans during the 1600s, when English, French, Spanish, and Dutch traders began offering them European industrial products in exchange for deerskins and beaver pelts.[16] Alcohol quickly became an integral part of the fur trade. Swedish and Finnish traders were carrying locally produced liquor to the Sámi communities by the 1590s.[17] Around the same time, English merchants introduced Caribbean rum to Native American towns on the Atlantic coast and farther west.[18]

Drinking acquired complex cultural meanings and social roles among Sámis and Shawnees alike. Among the Sámis, these aspects were documented extensively already in the late 1600s by Swedish missionaries. Crucially, most of these priests saw drinking as a normal part of social life rather than as a moral vice; some drank heavily themselves. Their depictions of Sámi practices are therefore largely neutral and quotidian in tone, suggesting that they are reasonably reliable.[19] According to the missionaries, alcohol was a valued luxury used to establish and maintain social relationships in Sámi communities. Gifts of liquor and collective drinking rituals during courtship and at weddings and funerals bound families and villages together. Alcohol was also shared generously with visitors.[20] What went unnoticed by the priests is that the extensive social networks liquor helped to create formed a vital safety net for Sámi families and villages, securing them access to the reindeer pastures, fishing sites, and hunting areas of allied communities and kin groups spread across the landscape. This made it easier to survive through annual and regional fluctuations in resources in the harsh northern environment.

Less is known about early Shawnee ways of drinking, as few literate colonists frequented Shawnee towns before the mid-1700s. Late eighteenth-century documents, however, make clear that Shawnee liquor consumption, too, had important ritual, social, and political dimensions. According to

British officers working with the Shawnees and American captives living in their communities, Shawnees sometimes consumed rum collectively at ceremonies. In particular, younger men drank heavily in military rituals. While meager, these documents imply that liquor lubricated the power of Shawnee war leaders who distributed intoxicants before military expeditions to encourage men to follow them.[21]

Native—newcomer relations, too, were negotiated by exchanging, sharing, and consuming alcohol. In Fennoscandia, small numbers of Swedish and Finnish farmers had settled on Sámi homelands since the Middle Ages; others made long fishing and hunting expeditions there every year. The Natives sought to integrate these newcomers and visitors in their social world on Indigenous terms. Local communities and families negotiated contracts with the southerners, giving them carefully specified rights to the Sámi land, water, and other resources.[22] There is fragmentary but interesting evidence that one element in such negotiations may have sometimes been gift-giving in which alcohol played a part. Some seventeenth-century court cases dealing with Sámi—colonist land disputes suggest that Swedish and Finnish settlers had provided Sámis with liquor and other rare goods, sometimes in repeated exchanges over a long period of time, in exchange for the right to settle on Native land or to use local resources.[23] Alcohol, then, offered the newcomers a point of entry into the Sámi country but entangled them in Native networks of reciprocal alliances based on sharing.

Sámis and Swedes employed alcohol also to articulate and debate the Natives' relationship with the expanding kingdom of Sweden. In the mid-1500s, Swedish elites began extending their power from what is now central and southern Sweden north to the Sámi country, hoping to gain control of the area's rich natural resources and to integrate the Natives into the kingdom as tribute-paying subjects. King Gustav Vasa declared royal protection over the Sámis and appointed officials to collect taxes and administer Swedish justice in their communities. The Lutheran Church, founded in Sweden by Vasa and led by his successors, initiated an aggressive missionary campaign to convert the Sámis and bind them into the spiritual community of the realm.[24] In early modern Europe, all these actions were understood as crucial steps in constructing sovereignty over subjects. What they actually meant in the Sámi country had to be negotiated in countless of everyday encounters, however. Far from metropolitan centers, crown officers and priests operating on Native homelands needed Sámi guides and their reindeer to travel across the wide and unfamiliar landscapes; furthermore, they depended on food procured by the Natives. The Sámis demanded payment for their services, frequently requesting alcohol from the officials.[25] Indeed, priests traveling in the Sámi country had to carry considerable stores of liquor with them and vicarages in the area became important centers of alcohol production and distribution.[26] When seen from the vantage point of Swedish–Sámi liquor exchanges, the Swedish kingdom on Native homelands appears not as a hegemonic colonial state but as a tentative network of reciprocal presents, services, rights, and obligations.

The complex roles of alcohol in the Sámi-Swedish negotiations crystallized in the establishment of special trading, administrative, and church centers known as marketplaces in the Sámi country. By the early seventeenth century the fur trade between the Sámis and the Swedes and Finns had become immensely important for both sides. Hoping to bring the trade more tightly under royal control, King Carl IX ordered in 1602 that all commerce with the Natives had to take place at prescribed times at sites sanctioned by crown officers. During the trade fairs the king's men would be present at these places to oversee the commerce, collect taxes from the Natives, and organize court sessions. Moreover, churches were to be built on the marketplaces and priests were to visit them during the trade fairs to teach Lutheranism to the Sámis. In short, the marketplaces were designed to become nodes of crown sovereignty where legal and spiritual rituals were to transform the Natives into legible subjects.[27]

In practice, however, the marketplaces became contested spaces where the Sámis and the Swedes used alcohol, among other things, to debate their relations. Swedish authorities had little power to force the Sámis to gather at the marketplaces at stated times; instead, they tried to attract the Natives to the trade fairs with generous distributions of food, beer, and liquor.[28] Moreover, both crown officers and independent merchants carried large amounts of alcohol to the marketplaces for trading. This made heavy drinking a prevalent activity during the trade fairs and eroded attempts to enforce Lutheran order at the marketplaces. Priests often complained that alcohol disrupted Christian teaching and promoted sinful practices during the fairs.[29] The Sámis, in contrast, seem to have understood the gatherings at the marketplaces as special festive occasions separated from the quotidian life by drunkenness and behavior not constrained by everyday social norms. Alcohol, then, turned the marketplaces into multivocal spaces that meant very different things to the Sámis and the Swedish officials. These sites, and the conflicting crown and Indigenous rituals enacted at them, constituted an important element in the rival Sámi and Swedish efforts to integrate one another into their competing social formations.

Alcohol mediated the relations between the Shawnees and the British in a similar fashion. To survive amid the geopolitical competition and warfare that ravaged eastern North America in the seventeenth century, Shawnee communities actively built alliances with the new English colonies springing up on the Atlantic coast. They found eager partners in Pennsylvania, New York, Carolina, and Maryland, all of whom needed Indian allies against their French colonial rivals and Native enemies.[30] Alliances between the Shawnees and the English were forged and maintained in highly ritualized councils, held in colonial cities or Native towns. Alcohol flowed profusely at these meetings. Sometimes the colonists welcomed Indian delegations arriving at the council site with "a Dram of Rum."[31] More commonly, they entertained the Native leaders with liquor and food in the evenings after the official business of the day had been closed, often sharing ceremonial toasts with them.[32] At the end of a council, the colonists delivered more alcohol to their allies as presents.[33]

Periodic gifts of liquor also bridged allied Shawnee and British communities separated by wide and potentially dangerous borderlands. Eager to maintain the allegiance of their Indian allies, the British frequently sent presents, including alcohol, to Shawnee towns. In 1731, for example, Pennsylvania's governor dispatched a trader from Philadelphia to the Shawnee communities on the Allegheny River to remind the Natives of their old friendship with the British and to warn them against allying with the French. Significantly, the messenger carried with him "some Liquor" to the Indians so that they would "remember [the Pennsylvanians] with Chearfulness."[34]

Yet, despite these common rituals of sharing alcohol, the Shawnees and the British interpreted gifts of liquor in dramatically different ways. The colonists believed that such gifts, together with other presents, were bribes necessary to buy the friendship of the supposedly mercenary Indians.[35] Sending alcohol to Shawnee towns was expected to tie the Natives to the political and economic orbit of the British empire. On a more symbolic level, drinking rituals in which Shawnee leaders "drank Prosperity to . . . the King of Great Britain, and the English Nation" allowed the colonists to imagine the Natives as vassal-like participants in their trans-Atlantic empire, subordinate to the crown but not members of the "English Nation."[36]

The Shawnees, on the other hand, believed that presents of liquor linked the English to Indigenous webs of alliance that were based on ceremonial kinship and reciprocal obligations rather than on a rigid hierarchy. They ritually adopted the king of England as their "father" and employed alcohol to instruct the colonists that, in the Native scheme of things, a father was a generous protector and provider whose duty was to always "be tender of his Children."[37] To drive home this point, many Shawnee leaders used gender-blending language that portrayed rum as the "milk" of their royal father. In 1795, for example, the headmen Catahecassa (Black Hoof) and Biaseka (Wolf) argued that the king's "Breasts" should always be "full of milk" for his Native children.[38] Gifts of alcohol, then, became a symbol of the care, generosity, and respect that Shawnees expected from their colonial allies.

Such expectations were not to be trifled with. If the British were stingy with liquor, the Shawnees complained that the king had forgotten his duties and was disregarding the alliance.[39] In 1765 the Haudenosaunee diplomat Kyashuta explained to crown officers that the Shawnees and other Ohio Valley nations had taken up arms against the British in the devastating Pontiac's War (1763–1765), because the colonists had "prohibited the sale of Powder, Lead, and Rum" to the Indians. In fact, British authorities had designed the ban to show to the Indians that their well-being depended on the empire. For the Shawnees, such a blatant refusal to share, or even sell, what were considered economic and social necessities amounted to a total breach of the alliance and justified violent retribution.[40] In eastern North America, then, alcohol came to epitomize the fundamental disagreement between Indians and colonists over who set the terms for international relations and whose understandings of power and alliances would weave together the continent's old and new inhabitants.

Regulation, Law, and Borders

Despite its manifold roles in international diplomacy and Native communal life, alcohol worried many Indigenous peoples and colonists on Sámi and Shawnee homelands. Due to its ability to produce powerful sensory effects and potentially disruptive behavior, Natives and newcomers recognized alcohol as a substance that required social regulation. Yet they often disagreed over who had the right to control it, where, and how. During the eighteenth century efforts to regulate liquor trade and consumption sparked conflicts over whose law would control traders and drinkers in which space. These debates took fundamentally dissimilar paths and imagined Indigenous status in divergent ways in northern Fennoscandia and eastern North America. In the former, it was the Swedish state-builders and priests who most vocally promoted alcohol regulation, and they did so in order to transform the Sámis into crown subjects and to enclose their country inside the borders of the kingdom. In the Shawnee country, alcohol control was driven primarily by the Shawnee leadership in an effort to suppress social problems and consolidate national authority. Both Shawnees and British situated the Indians outside the legal and political boundaries of the British empire; however, while the Shawnee liquor regulators envisioned a separate Shawnee homeland under full Shawnee sovereignty, the colonists denied that the Natives could hold authority over crown subjects and their activities, such as alcohol trade, even in the Indian country.

The view that Sámi drinking was something the state should regulate was first voiced in Sweden in 1686, when Mathias Steuchius, a representative of the clergy at the Estates, declared that the Natives were "corrupting them-selves completely with spirits."[41] Steuchius made his exaggerated claim as a part of an emerging debate about the dangers of alcohol. The production and use of liquor had grown exponentially in Sweden over the seventeenth cen-tury, making some clergymen concerned about the influence of drinking on public morality.[42] Crown officials, too, worried about alcohol, although their reasons were mostly connected to state finances and geopolitics. Through-out the kingdom, peasants used so much of their crops for producing spir-its that the government had to import large amounts of cereals each year. This, in turn, diverted money from other state projects, such as maintaining the army.[43]

Motivated by such diverse agendas, the Swedish government began po-licing alcohol throughout the kingdom in the early 1700s. The production of liquor was periodically banned and public drunkenness criminalized.[44] While the state control targeted all subjects, especially the lower classes, the Sámis faced complex special regulations. Priests were instructed to fine Natives who appeared intoxicated on the Sabbath,[45] and in 1723 the crown prohibited the sale of liquor at the marketplaces during the trade fairs until the official part of the gatherings had been finished.[46]

Some Swedes, however, saw alcohol regulation in the Sámi country as a geopolitical threat that undermined the kingdom. Merchants in the northern towns heavily dependent on Sámi trade protested that banning liquor drove the Natives to trade and live in Norway, where inebriants were controlled less severely.[47] Some Sámis likewise criticized the crown's efforts to inter-fere in their drinking, which was, after all, a socially important activity. In 1733, for example, unidentified Sámis from the Ohcejohka (Utsjoki) commu-nity explained that for them alcohol was a much-needed "medicine"—a com-mon usage throughout Europe at the time—and protested that anyone "who use[d] such gifts of God otherwise" could only "blame himself."[48]

Crown officers took the displeasure of the Sámis and the merchants' warnings seriously, for they feared a large-scale migration of the Natives out of the kingdom. Even seasonal Sámi trading expeditions to Norway worried state officials, as such journeys drained specie, furs, and other valuables out of Sweden.[49] Even worse, permanent out-migrations threatened to rob the kingdom of valuable taxpayers and jeopardized its territorial claims. Swe-den, Denmark—Norway, and Russia based their competing claims in the Sámi homelands on claims of sovereignty over the Sámis, demonstrated by col-lecting taxes from the Natives, administering justice among them, and build-ing churches in their communities.[50] Therefore, if large numbers of Sámis had moved west, broken their ties with Swedish officials and priests, and integrated within the Dano-Norwegian networks of justice, taxation, and worship, Sweden's claims in the north would have been seriously weakened.[51] Under such pressures, crown officials actually *relaxed* statewide alcohol restrictions on Sámi homelands time and again during the 1700s.[52]

Liquor produced perennial problems for the Swedish campaign to consolidate state sovereignty and borders in the Sámi country. At the same time, it lubricated Native efforts to maintain autonomous Indigenous spaces amid growing state encroachments. In 1751 Sweden and Denmark—Norway concluded the Treaty of Strömstad, which for the first time defined an exact boundary between the two kingdoms. The new border cut through Sámi homelands, dividing traditional reindeer herding routes, hunting grounds, and kinship networks into nominally Swedish and Dano-Norwegian territories. The Natives retained a right to cross the boundary unhindered, however.[53] This allowed them to use alcohol to contest the political geography imposed on them by the states. Whenever Sweden attempted to restrict the liquor trade within its boundaries, many Sámis simply crossed the new border to Norway to buy alcohol there. They then circulated and shared the liquor among their friends, relatives, and allies to expand and solidify connections between families and villages stretching from the "Norwegian" coast of the Atlantic deep into the "Swedish" inland. In 1763, for example, the Swedish vicar of Ohcejohka lamented that the local Sámis were often drunk, because they could easily procure liquor on the Norwegian side of the border that ran through the traditional lands of the community.[54] That the Ohcejohka people continued to carry alcohol across the border and drink it on the "Swedish" side shows that they still saw the landscape as their own space, defined by their patterns of travel, exchange, and social relationships, rather than as a territory regulated by Swedish lines and laws.

If liquor control in the Sámi country was largely a colonial technology for building state power, among the Shawnees it was an anticolonial project. On Shawnee homelands, it was the Native leaders who first sought to regulate alcohol trade and consumption. By the early eighteenth century several Shawnee headmen were voicing their concerns about what they deemed excessive liquor consumption among their people. Some protested that colonial traders cheated Native hunters after first intoxicating them with liberal gifts of alcohol.[55] Even more disturbingly, others argued that drinking led to unprecedented levels of violence in their communities. In 1738, for instance, the headmen Nucheconner, Coyacolinne, and Laypareawah from the Allegheny River contended that the "Drinking of Rum" had produced "ill Consequances" in their towns, including the violent deaths of two Haudenosaunee visitors.[56] Drunken brawls posed a serious problem in Shawnee communities, where leaders were expected to keep the peace with only "fair words" and possessed few means beyond persuasion to foster social harmony.[57]

Due to that consensual nature of their authority, Shawnee leaders initially found it difficult to compel their people to stop drinking alcohol. Instead, they demanded British authorities to stop the colonists from selling liquor, claiming that the root cause of the problem was colonial supply, not Native demand.[58] Few Britons were eager to restrict the trade, however, for alcohol commerce was a lucrative business.[59] Even when colonial elites passed laws to curtail the commerce, enforcing the legislation proved difficult. In 1721 Pennsylvania's governor explained to Shawnees and their neighbors that "the Country is so wide, [and] the woods are so dark and private, and so far out of my sight" that he could not stop colonial traders from carrying alcohol to Native homelands. His successor lamented that the liquor trade was "carry'd on in the Woods, and at such a Distance from the Seat of Government" that it was "very difficult" to bring the culprits to justice.[60]

These arguments crystallized key strands in the nascent British thinking about Native American status and place. Unlike the Swedes, the British drew a sharp line between Native and colonial territories and jurisdictions. Although monarchs and political theorists in Europe often claimed crown sovereignty over much of North America, on the ground colonial officials admitted that British authority and law did not reach into the "dark" and distant Indian country. Yet they vehemently denied the possibility that British subjects venturing there could fall under Indigenous law. Pennsylvanian officials, for example, instructed the leaders of the Shawnees and their neighbors to make "Laws against [their own people] drinking" alcohol, not against the colonists selling it.[61] In the British imagination, then, the Indian country became a space of shared sovereignty where Native laws and authorities governed Native communities, while British subjects remained under colonial jurisdiction, no matter how inefficient.

In the 1730s, Shawnee chiefs contested this vision to assert total Native sovereignty over the Indian country. Concerned about the "Disturbance" colonial rum was breeding in their communities, Nucheconner and other leaders of three Shawnee towns on the Allegheny and Ohio rivers launched an ambitious program to regulate the liquor trade. In 1738 they prohibited alcohol in their communities and "Oppointed four men to Stave all the Rum" brought in.[62] The prohibition demonstrated a new centralized and territorialized vision of Shawnee sovereignty as chiefly authority over the landscape and all the people moving through it. Importantly, this vision emerged in a wider context of Shawnee leaders consolidating their nation and defining its borders between the expanding British and French empires.[63] The alcohol ban was short-lived, however: within a few years all references to it vanished from the British documents. Many Shawnees, accustomed to considerable clan autonomy, may have resented the chiefs' efforts to interfere in their trading and drinking so much that the leaders had to abandon their regulatory program.

Despite the apparent failure of this early prohibition, some Shawnee communities later instituted similar programs of liquor control. Many more continued to request colonial authorities to curtail the alcohol trade.[64] Rather than support the Shawnee efforts, however, the British actively undermined them. This is demonstrated most vividly by the British interpretations of the Royal Proclamation of 1763. The Proclamation was designed to address the legacies of the Anglo-French Seven Years' War (1756–1763), which had ended in France surrendering to Great Britain all its clams to the lands between the Appalachian Mountains and the Mississippi River. The British government crafted the Royal Proclamation to clarify the status of this territory and the Indian nations controlling it. Most famously, the Proclamation divided North America into British and Indian territories along the Appalachians and forbade, for the time being, colonial settlements west of the mountains.[65]

The Royal Proclamation boundary replicated the long-standing British idea of a strict separation between Native and colonial lands. However, the border was far from watertight. Indeed, imperial officials allowed British traders and alcohol to cross it freely into the Indian country. When the crown's superintendent of Indian affairs, Sir William Johnson, sketched future British Indian policy in 1764, he stressed how important this was for imperial interests. Johnson believed that the fur trade made Indians economically dependent on the empire and forced them to submit to British rule. Alcohol, in turn, was essential to the trade. Johnson claimed that the Natives had a relatively limited need of most colonial products but an insatiable thirst for rum. Therefore, if the British respected Indigenous efforts to restrict the alcohol commerce, "the Trade will never be so Extensive" and effective in producing Native dependency as with rum. It was, Johnson argued, "absolutely necessary" to allow the liquor traffic regardless of Native opinions.[66]

International law, as it was understood in Europe in the eighteenth century, recognized the right of states to restrict or even ban foreign imports. Influenced by mercantilist economic theories, Great Britain regularly placed restrictions on imports considered harmful or superfluous.[67] Both European theorists and colonial officials, however, denied that Shawnees or other Native Americans, not organized into what Europeans recognized as states, possessed similar rights.[68] That British authorities promoted the free trade of alcohol in the Indian country regardless of the opinion of Native leadership demonstrates that they did not regard the Shawnees and their neighbors as fully sovereign peoples in control of sovereign territories. Neither were Native borders accorded the same respect as European ones; instead, they were conceptualized as porous lines that could be crossed by colonial traders and goods with little formal reference to Indian authorities.

Civilization, Race, and Nation

In the early nineteenth century, alcohol became enmeshed in two competing colonial constructions of Indigenous status in both Fennoscandia and North America. Briefly, at issue was whether it was possible to integrate the Natives into the settler states through programs of cultural assimilation and religious conversion. While some government officials, missionaries, and others in North America and Fennoscandia alike advocated "civilizing" the Natives, others insisted that the Indians and the Sámis constituted separate races so different from "white" Europeans and Euro-Americans that they could never be assimilated and had to instead be segregated to state margins.

The supporters of each view made alcohol a central part of their arguments. In Sweden, efforts to civilize and Christianize the Sámis had motivated state attempts to control Sámi alcohol consumption since the seventeenth century. The young United States launched its own civilization program in the 1790s in an effort to integrate Native Americans into the republic. Among other things, this meant policing the Indians' liquor use. Federal officials deemed drunkenness incompatible with republican citizenship and, from 1802 on, began limiting Indigenous access to alcohol.[69]

These civilization programs stemmed from a conviction that assimilating Native peoples into the colonial culture and population was possible. However, at the turn of the nineteenth century the rising ideology of race contributed to a diametrically opposite belief, which held that fundamental racial differences separated the Natives from the colonists and made it difficult, perhaps impossible, for the two groups to live together. Liquor lubricated colonial constructions of Indigenous peoples as racial Others on the opposite sides of the Atlantic. Ever since the seventeenth century some British and Swedes had drawn attention to the alleged differences between colonial and Native drinking habits. Such views seem to have become more common during the eighteenth century. British elites, for example, believed that while they mastered a civilized "art of getting drunk," the Indians turned "beasts" when intoxicated.[70] Swedish priests and officials, in turn, evoked words like "crazy" and "mad" to describe drunken Sámis.[71] Similarly, the colonists believed that the Natives' yearning for alcohol exceeded all normal limits and was based more on nature than nurture. When Swedes insisted in the 1740s that the Sámis were "such a people that has no restraint when it comes to drinking" and a Pennsylvanian official claimed in 1762 that "Indians cannot be kept from drink," they all portrayed the Natives as a separate category of humans, physically and psychologically different from the whites.[72] By the early nineteenth century, colonists in North America and Fennoscandia alike took it for granted that "excessive ebriety" among the Indians and the Sámis was not "an individual characteristic" but a "passion" or "love" that characterized these Native races in general.[73]

In each region race intertwined with emerging nationalism. Through the nineteenth century, Europeans and Euro-Americans used "race" and "nation" as rough synonyms and conceptualized nationhood in racial, as well as cultural, terms as shared customs, language, origins, mentality, and physical characteristics.[74] For state-builders in the United States, Sweden, and Finland, alcohol abuse, an alleged racial "passion" of Indians and Sámis, became a powerful symbol for distinguishing the Indigenous peoples from the American, Swedish, and Finnish nations and for defining the Natives as a special category of people under state authority but lacking the rights of citizens or subjects. In each country, officials agreed that the excessive Indigenous taste for strong drinks necessitated government interference in Native affairs. In particular, drinking was portrayed as a hindrance to Indian and Sámi civilization and economic progress. Through the early nineteenth century, Finnish newspapers, for instance, abounded with stories about unscrupulous traders who cheated intoxicated Sámis of "all of their tools and morsels of food."[75] In the United States, federal officials argued that if the Shawnees and their neighbors did not waste time on "drinking and frolicking," they "would soon make a good living."[76] Such language construed the Indigenous peoples as economically poor and mentally immature dependents in need of paternal state control.

Despite these basic similarities, the state governments envisioned their Indigenous wards' place in the national, racial, and legal landscape very differently on the opposite sides of the Atlantic. In the United States, alcohol intertwined with the Indian Removal, a massive project designed to segregate the Indian "Others" from the "white" citizens. By the 1820s, Americans widely supported the plan of resettling the Native nations living on the east side of the Mississippi to the territory west of the river, an area envisioned as a permanent Indian country.[77] Racializing images of drunken Indians formed an important element in the pro-removal discourses. Time and again, removal advocates insisted that Indians could never be civilized in close proximity of American settlements where they had a constant access to alcohol. Liquor's "wasting influence" allegedly "depraved" the Natives and decimated their numbers, making it crucial to segregate them from U.S. citizens.[78] Motivated, in part, by such arguments, the federal government forced nearly eighty thousand Natives, including about one thousand Shawnees, to remove across the Mississippi in the 1830s and 1840s.[79]

In 1832 and 1834 Congress, seeking to solidify federal control over the Indian country and its newly removed residents, enacted complex legislation that curtailed the sale of alcohol in the area.[80] The new laws represented a mixture of tribal sovereignty and federal power. They made it illegal for non-Indians to sell alcohol to the Natives in the Indian country, but left Indigenous consumption and trade of liquor there under tribal sovereignty. This continued the old British tradition of envisioning Native American homelands as spaces of shared sovereignty. The federal liquor laws imagined an Indian country where semiautonomous Native nations lived partially inside, partially outside U.S. jurisdiction but lacked any legal authority over American citizens.

Fennoscandian states constructed the status of the Sámis and their homelands in a different manner. Finland, long the eastern province of the kingdom of Sweden, was annexed to the Russian empire as an autonomous grand duchy in 1809. As one part in the long process of consolidating law and administration in this new political and national entity, in 1838 Finland's senate banned the production and sale of liquor in the Sámi country and organized the region, known as Lapland, into a new jurisdictional district, almost doubling the number of sheriffs there.[81] The next year Sweden similarly outlawed alcohol in its province of Lapland.[82] Unlike U.S. legislation, these laws recognized no Indigenous sovereignty over alcohol trade and use. Nor were they initially race-based: both Finnish and Swedish alcohol bans applied to all residents of the two Lapland provinces, whether Natives or non-Natives. Whereas U.S. authorities saw Indians as distinct nations living on separate homelands, Swedish and Finnish officials defined the Sámis as a racial minority within the states.

Shawnee and Sámi strategies for dealing with the state-imposed liquor regulations were also radically different. Among the Shawnees, the U.S. ban became a site of complex internal and external struggles for power. Relocated to a reservation in what is now eastern Kansas in the 1830s, the Shawnees faced a powerful onslaught of American inebriants. Just across the reservation's eastern border, in Missouri (significantly *outside* the Indian country), distilling alcohol was growing into a thriving industry and most local producers marketed their liquor among the thousands of removed Indians living in the vicinity.[83] Drinking divided the Shawnees. Some, especially young men, regularly bought alcohol from Missouri, often consuming it in "a spirit of bravado" to "show [the federal officials] that they disregard[ed] their threats."[84] Others, in contrast, sought new methods for suppressing liquor and the evils it was perceived to create. After the removal, some Shawnee families had begun to transform their traditional subsistence economy toward a more commercial agriculture. By the 1840s a few of these families had become relatively wealthy, and gradually they assumed political leadership on the reservation as well.[85] This new elite saw alcohol as a multifaceted political and economic problem. They were well aware that U.S. officials constantly evoked stereo-typical images of drunken Indians to limit Native sovereignty.[86] In addition, some wealthy Shawnees were opposed to alcohol, because "the drunkards & idle" among their tribespeople reportedly killed their hogs, ate their corn, and left debts unpaid, disturbing their commercial activities.[87]

In 1852 the new Shawnee elite established the National Council to govern the reservation.[88] The council quickly tightened its grip on alcohol and crafted laws to provide the reservation leadership with methods for disciplining intoxicated young men and collecting debts from drunkards.[89] In addition, the National Council began to administer the annuity shares of those tribal members it defined as drunkards; these monies were kept by a trustee appointed by the council.[90] Alcohol, then, fueled new forms of power based on centralized national authority and an incipient capitalist economy.

The authority of the National Council remained limited, however. While it claimed power over the Shawnees on the reservation, it lacked legal means to regulate the activities of American liquor traders, whether on- or off-reservation. American constructions of Indian sovereignty made the council's authority narrowly race-based and continued to deny full territorial sovereignty from the Shawnee nation.

Just like in North America, in the Sámi country many Natives continued to drink and trade liquor despite the Finnish and Swedish prohibitions. However, since the late eighteenth century some Sámis had been voicing concerns that alcohol was undermining the social fabric and economic base of their communities.[91] As Finnish and Swedish law recognized no Sámi sovereignty nor any Indigenous institutions that could have practiced autonomy, Native efforts to control alcohol found an outlet in Christianity. Lutheran priests had long complained that drinking impeded the conversion and civilization of the Sámis. In the early nineteenth century they found growing numbers of adherents among the Natives. When priests portrayed alcohol as a satanic force that tempted people to sin, many Sámis who had seen too many drunken brawls and families impoverished by liquor agreed. Local temperance movements, often organized by priests, began to spring up across the Sámi country in the 1840s.[92] The most influential promoter of temperance was Lars Levi Laestadius, a Lutheran priest with a Sámi background. A powerful orator, Laestadius mixed Christianity with Sámi spirituality in his teaching, describing the Devil as "that staalo [a traditional Sámi monster] of liquor" who "burns the souls of drunkards in a brimstone lake." Laestadius's message spread rapidly among the Sámis in the 1840s and 1850s, encouraging many to leave drinking altogether.[93]

Occasionally Sámi temperance activism assumed an aggressively anti-colonial character. In 1852 a group of Sámis inspired by Laestadius's teachings killed a liquor trader and the local sheriff in Guovdageaidnu (Kautokeino).[94] This was a unique event, however. Usually the Sámis relied on state officials to control the alcohol trade and sought quietly among themselves to solve the problems created by drinking. For example, between 1860 and 1910 only five Sámis were convicted of drunkenness or other alcohol-related crimes in the community of Jåhkåmåhkke (Jokkmokk), Sweden.[95] The low number implies that the locals intentionally kept all but the most serious cases of drunken misbehavior outside the Swedish courts.

The Sámi temperance movements did not bring about a universal end to Indigenous drinking. Alcohol trade and consumption persisted through the mid-1800s and, like before, they were often connected to Sámi transborder mobility. For state officials, this represented a multifaceted problem that threatened both the states' power to control their boundaries and the governments' efforts to civilize the Natives. For example, in 1833 Finnish officials accused "Norwegian Lapps" of visiting Finnish territory with spirits and corrupting the local Natives.[96] Similarly, when the Ohcejohka Sámis from Finland continued to travel to Norway and purchase liquor there, the local sheriff protested that this turned "our Finnish Lapps" "untamed."[97]

Such language construed the Sámis as members of the Fennoscandian nation-states but defined them a special group of subjects. Evolving liquor legislation, too, continued to place the Natives in an ambiguous position somewhere between insiders and outsiders. During the second half of the nineteenth century the alcohol laws of both Finland and Sweden became increasingly race-based and began to differentiate the Sámis from the Finnish and Swedish inhabitants of the Lapland provinces. For example, in 1858 Finland allowed the non-Natives living in Lapland to import limited amounts of liquor to the area for household consumption, while Sámi alcohol consumption remained entirely banned. Sweden, in turn, later prohibited selling intoxicating beverages to the Sámis even outside the province of Lapland.[98] Increasingly, both countries used alcohol regulation to bring the Natives under state control while excluding them from the racially constructed Finnish and Swedish nations.

Conclusions

A comparative history of alcohol consumption and control on Shawnee and Sámi homelands not only illuminates the multiple connections between liquor and colonialism but also casts into sharp relief an even more profound historical process: the development of diverse visions of Indigenous status and place in the colonial world. Juxtaposing the Shawnee and Sámi histories of alcohol use and regulation complicates standard accounts of this process and its outcomes in each region. While U.S. histories have emphasized violent colonial conquest that pushed Native Americans *outside* the emerging settler state, Swedish and Finnish narratives have stressed the peaceful integration of the Sámis *inside* state structures and spaces. Cross-examining Shawnee and Sámi experiences with liquor, however, demonstrates how confused and contradictory colonial policies and ideologies actually were.

In Fennoscandia and North America alike, colonial alcohol trade and regulation, as well discourses about liquor, defined Indigenous peoples simultaneously as real or potential subjects and as outsiders, and located them both inside and outside colonial structures and spaces. From early on, the British situated the Shawnees and their Native neighbors outside British law. Similarly, they evoked the allegedly uncivilized Indian drinking habits to define the Natives as racial Others, something that later formed an important argument for segregating the Indigenous nations from U.S. citizens through the Indian Removal program. Yet neither the British nor their American successors ever acknowledged full Indigenous sovereignty even in the Indian country, as demonstrated by their reluctance to accept that Native laws and authorities could regulate the liquor trade on Native homelands. On the contrary, both British and Americans believed themselves entitled to ban or allow alcohol in the Indian country.

In the Sámi country, on the other hand, Sweden used alcohol legislation to define the Natives as crown subjects and the Native homelands as a part of the kingdom already in the seventeenth century. However, the king's officials, concerned about a potential out-migration of the Sámis, often relaxed statewide liquor restrictions in the Sámi country and allowed the Natives to import intoxicants from Norway. In addition, in the nineteenth century both Swedish and Finnish alcohol legislation constructed the Sámis simultaneously as state subjects and as racial outsiders fundamentally different from the Swedes and Finns.

These contradictions and inconsistences imply that colonial statebuilders on both sides of the Atlantic found Native peoples problematic. The Natives defied easy categorization within the rapidly evolving European and colonial political imaginations. From the seventeenth through the nineteenth century, nascent ideologies of territorial sovereignty, race, and nationalism transformed how Europeans and their colonial descendants across the globe conceptualized political community and political geography, prompting them to ask where the Indigenous peoples belonged in a landscape increasingly envisioned as a patchwork of bounded, consolidated, and ethnically unified states. The confusing British, American, Swedish, and Finnish policies of alcohol commerce and control demonstrate that the colonists never found unambiguous solutions to this conundrum. Consequently, Indigenous peoples came to occupy "an uncertain position" in colonial political structures and imaginations, and colonial constructions of Indigeneity began to take shape as an inherently contradictory category of people permanently locked somewhere between insiders and outsiders.[99]

Analyzing the Sámi and Shawnee cases side by side further complicates this picture, because the Natives employed alcohol to articulate their own visions of status, place, and belonging. Based on dissimilar cultural constructions of drinking and variegated geopolitical strategies, these visions could both challenge the colonial ones and merge with them. Initially, Sámis and Shawnees alike used alcohol to integrate the colonists into their social networks and landscapes on their own terms. Rather than separating outsiders from insiders, they exchanged and drank liquor to transform the former into the latter. However, from the 1730s on, the Shawnee leadership made liquor regulation an important part of their fiercely anticolonial program of national and territorial consolidation that rested on drawing political and legal borders between Indians and Euro-Americans. The Sámis, on the other hand, drank and shared alcohol to build and reproduce Indigenous social and economic networks that crossed colonial borders and maintained autonomous Native geographies. Faced with settler-colonialism, the Shawnees made liquor a vehicle of their own insider/outsider divisions, while the Sámis, navigating economic exploitation and political incorporation, used alcohol to confuse the strict boundaries and binary categories imposed on them by the colonial states.

SAMI LAKOMÄKI is a university lecturer of cultural anthropology at the University of Oulu.

RITVA KYLLI is a docent and a university lecturer of history at the University of Oulu.

TIMO YLIMAUNU is a docent and a university lecturer of archaeology at University of Oulu, as well as an international associate at Indiana University—Purdue University Indianapolis.

Notes

1. Roger Kvist, "Samerna och alkoholen: Jokkmokks socken, 1760–1860," *Alkoholpolitik: Tidskrift för nordisk alkoholforskning* 3, no. 3 (1986): 122–28 (information from 123); *Samling af Placater, Förordningar, Manifester och Påbud,*

samt andre Allmänna Handlingar, hwilka i Stor-Furstendömet Finland sedan 1808 års början ifrån trycket utkommit: Vol. 7, 1835—1838 (Helsingfors: G. O. Wasenius, 1840), 319—22; William E. Unrau, *White Man's Wicked Water: The Alcohol Trade and Prohibition in Indian Country, 1802—1892* (Lawrence: University Press of Kansas, 1996), 37.

2. Geoffrey Hunt and Judith C. Barker, "Socio-cultural Anthropology and Alcohol and Drug Research: Toward a Unified Theory," *Social Science and Medicine* 53, no. 2 (2001): 165—85 ("colonizing . . ." from page 182); Unrau, *White Man's Wicked Water*, 12 ("particularly . . ." from page 12); Michael Dietler, "Alcohol: Anthropological/Archaeological Perspectives," *Annual Review of Anthropology* 35 (2006): 229—49 ("complex . . ." from page 239).

3. Emmanuel Kwaku Akyeampong, *Drink, Power, and Cultural Change: A Social History of Alcohol in Ghana, c. 1800 to Recent Times* (Portsmouth, N.H.: Heinemann, 1996); David Carey Jr., ed., *Distilling the Influence of Alcohol: Aguardiente in Guatemalan History* (Gainesville: University Press of Florida, 2012); Izumi Ishii, "Alcohol and Politics in the Cherokee Nation before Removal," *Ethnohistory* 50, no. 4 (2003): 671—95; Justin Willis, *Potent Brews: A Social History of Alcohol in East Africa, 1850—1999* (London: British Institute in Eastern Africa, 2002). The scholarship on alcohol and colonialism has largely focused on Africa. For brief studies on the history of alcohol among the Sámis, see Kvist, "Samerna och alkoholen"; Roger Kvist, "Nomadic Saami and Alcohol: Jokkmokk Parish, 1760—1910," *Canadian Journal of Native Studies* 12, no. 2 (1992): 185—201; Roger Kvist, "Myten om samerna och alkoholen," *Spiritus: Skriftserie från Vin & spirithistoriska museet* 6 (2004): 1—13; Peter Sköld and Roger Kvist, "Alkoholen och de nomadiserande samerna: Jokkmokks socken, 1860—1910," *Alkoholpolitik: Tidskrift för nordisk alkoholforskning* 5, no. 4 (1988): 249—54; Peter Sköld, "Seime staembe: Brännvinet i den samiska religionen," *Oknytt* 20, nos. 1—4 (1999): 63—84. No study focuses exclusively on Shawnee histories of alcohol consumption and control, but two more general monographs on Native Americans and alcohol utilize a lot of Shawnee material: Peter C. Mancall, *Deadly Medicine: Indians and Alcohol in Early America* (Ithaca, N.Y.: Cornell University Press, 1995); and Unrau, *White Man's Wicked Water.*

4. Akyeampong, *Drink, Power, and Cultural Change*; David Carey, Jr., "Introduction: Writing the History of Alcohol in Guatemala," in *Distilling the Influence of Alcohol*, ed. Carey, 1—16; Jonathan Crush and Charles Ambler, eds., *Liquor and Labor in Southern Africa* (Athens: Ohio University Press, 1992); Susan Diduk, "European Alcohol, History, and the State in Cameroon," *African Studies Review* 36, no. 10 (1993): 1—42; Dietler, "Alcohol"; Ishii, "Alcohol and Politics in the Cherokee Nation"; Mancall, *Deadly Medicine*; Lynn Pan, *Alcohol in Colonial Africa* (Helsinki: Finnish Foundation for Alcohol Studies, 1975); Franz Scaramelli and Kay Tarble de Scaramelli, "The Roles of Material Culture in the Colonization of the Orinoco, Venezuela," *Journal of Social Archaeology* 5, no. 1 (2005): 135—68; Frederick H. Smith, *Caribbean Rum: A Social and Economic History* (Gainesville: University Press of Florida, 2005); Unrau, *White Man's Wicked Water*; Willis, *Potent Brews.*

5. Sami Lakomäki, "Globalizing Indigenous Histories: Comparison, Connect-

edness, and New Contexts for Native American History," in *Twenty-First Century Perspectives on Indigenous Studies: Native North America in (Trans)Motion*, eds. Birgit Däwes, Karsten Fitz, and Sabine N. Meyer (New York: Routledge, 2015), 187–203; Mark Peterson, "Indians and the National Narrative: The Trouble with Words and with Us," *William and Mary Quarterly* 69, no. 3 (2012): 531–34.

6. Colin G. Calloway, "2008 Presidential Address: Indian History from the End of the Alphabet; And What Now?" *Ethnohistory* 58, no. 2 (2011): 197–211 (quotations from page 201); Ken S. Coates, *A Global History of Indigenous Peoples: Struggle and Survival* (New York: Palgrave Macmillan, 2004).

7. Matt Daunton and Rick Halpern, eds., *Empire and Others: British Encounters with Indigenous Peoples, 1600–1850* (Philadelphia: University of Pennsylvania Press, 1999); Gunlög Fur, *Colonialism in the Margins: Cultural Encounters in New Sweden and Lapland* (Leiden: Brill, 2006); James O. Gump, *The Dust Rose Like Smoke: The Subjugation of the Zulu and the Sioux* (Lincoln: University of Nebraska Press, 1994); Katrina Jagodinsky, *Legal Codes and Talking Trees: Indigenous Women's Sovereignty in the Sonoran and Puget Sound Borderlands, 1854–1946* (New Haven, Conn.: Yale University Press, 2016); Lakomäki, "Globalizing Indigenous Histories"; David Maybury-Lewis, Theodore Macdonald, and Biorn Maybury-Lewis, eds., *Manifest Destinies and Indigenous Peoples* (Cambridge, Mass.: Harvard University Press, 2009); Angela Wanhalla, "Women 'Living across the Line': Intermarriage on the Canadian Prairies and in Southern New Zealand, 1870–1900," *Ethnohistory* 55, no. 1 (2008): 29–49; Patrick Wolfe, "Settler Colonialism and the Elimination of the Native," *Journal of Genocide Research* 8, no. 4 (2006): 387–409. A related field investigates European colonialisms from a comparative perspective. See, for example, Lauren Benton, *A Search for Sovereignty: Law and Geography in European Empires, 1400–1900* (Cambridge, U.K.: Cambridge University Press, 2010); J. H. Elliott, *Empires of the Atlantic World: Britain and Spain in America, 1492–1830* (New Haven, Conn.: Yale University Press, 2006); Ann Laura Stoler, "Tense and Tender Ties: The Politics of Comparison in North American History and (Post) Colonial Studies," *Journal of American History* 88, no. 3 (2001): 829–65.

8. Gary Clayton Anderson, *Ethnic Cleansing and the Indian: The Crime That Should Haunt America* (Norman: University of Oklahoma Press, 2014); Colin G. Calloway, *The Shawnees and the War for America* (New York: Viking, 2007); Sami Lakomäki, *Gathering Together: The Shawnee People through Diaspora and Nationhood, 1600–1870* (New Haven, Conn.: Yale University Press, 2014); Stephen Warren, *The Shawnees and Their Neighbors, 1795–1870* (Urbana: University of Illinois Press, 2005); Stephen Warren, *The Worlds the Shawnees Made: Migration and Violence in Early America* (Chapel Hill: University of North Carolina Press, 2014).

9. Lars Ivar Hansen and Bjørnar Olsen, *Samenes historie fram til 1750* (Oslo: Cappelen Akademisk Forlag, 2004), 150–353; Karin Granqvist, *Samerna, staten och rätten i Torne lappmark under 1600-talet: Makt, diskurs och representation* (Umeå: Umeå universitet, 2004); Håkan Rydving, "The End of Drum-Time: Religious Change among the Lule Saami, 1670s–1740s" (Ph.D. diss., Uppsala University, 1993).

10. For the long-standing scholarly interest in warfare in Shawnee history, see Calloway, *Shawnees and the War for America*, xxii; Warren, *Shawnees and Their Neighbors*, 15; Pekka Hämäläinen, *The Comanche Empire* (New Haven, Conn.: Yale University Press, 2008), 1 (quotation).

11. For the traditional view, see e.g. Sune Åkerman, "Bondesamhälle och samesamhälle under senmedeltiden och tidig nyare tid," in *Stat, religion, etnisitet*, eds. Bjørn-Petter Finstad, Lars Ivar Hansen, Henry Minde, Einar Niemi, and Hallvard Tjelmeland (Tromsø: Sámi dutkamiid guovddáš, 1997), 341–81 ("peaceful" from 347); Matti Enbuske, *Vanhan Lapin valtamailla: Asutus ja maankäyttö Kemin Lapin ja Enontekiön alueella 1500-luvulta 1900-luvun alkuun* (Helsinki: SKS, 2008); Maria Lähteenmäki, *Kalotin kansaa: Rajankäynnit ja vuorovaikutus Pohjoiskalotilla, 1808–1889* (Helsinki: SKS, 2004). For critical voices, see, for example, Lars Anders Baer, "Inledningsanförande: Samisk forskning i en postcolonial diskurs," in *Människor i norr: Samisk forskning på nya vägar*, ed. Peter Sköld (Umeå: Vaartoe–Centrum för Samisk forskning, Umeå universitet, 2008), 21–27; Gunlög Fur, "Colonialism and Swedish History: Unthinkable Connections?" in *Scandinavian Colonialism and the Rise of Modernity: Small Time Agents in a Global Arena*, eds. Magdalena Naum and Jonas M. Nordin (New York: Springer, 2013), 17–36 ("integration" from 25); Magdalena Naum and Jonas M. Nordin, "Introduction: Situating Scandinavian Colonialism," in *Scandinavian Colonialism and the Rise of Modernity*, eds. Naum and Nordin, 3–16; Carl-Gösta Ojala, *Sámi Prehistories: The Politics of Archaeology and Identity in Northernmost Europe* (Uppsala: Institutet för arkeologi och antic historia, Uppsala universitet, 2009), 89, 92.

12. For example, Allan Greer, "Dispossession in a Commercial Idiom: From Indian Deeds to Land Cession Treaties," in *Contested Spaces of Early America*, eds. Juliana Barr and Edward Countryman (Philadelphia: University of Pennsylvania Press, 2014), 69–92.

13. For example, Enbuske, *Vanhan Lapin valtamailla*; Ojala, *Sámi Prehistories*, 89; Trond Thuen, "Cultural Policies on the North Calotte," *Acta Borealia* 19, no. 2 (2002): 147–64.

14. Benedict Anderson, *Imagined Communities: Reflections of the Origin and Spread of Nationalism* (London: Verso, 1991); Thomas Biolsi, "Imagined Geographies: Sovereignty, Indigenous Space, and American Indian Struggle," *American Ethnologist* 32, no. 2 (2005): 239–59; Kimmo Katajala, "Maps, Borders, and State-Building," in *Physical and Cultural Space in Pre-industrial Europe: Methodological Approaches to Spatiality*, eds. Marko Lamberg, Marko Hakanen, and Janne Haikari (Lund: Nordic Academic Press, 2011), 58–91.

15. Hansen and Olsen, *Samenes historie*, 136–39, 155–64.

16. Daniel K. Richter, *Facing East from Indian Country: A Native History of Early America* (Cambridge, Mass.: Harvard University Press, 2001), 42–53.

17. Isak Fellman, ed., *Handlingar och uppsatser angående finska lappmarken och lapparne*, vol. 4 (Helsingfors: Finska Litteratursällskapets tryckeri, 1915), 50, 54, 56.

18. Mancall, *Deadly Medicine*, 41–43.

19. Kvist, "Myten om samerna," 3.

20. Samuele Rheen, "En kortt Relation om Lapparnes Lefwarne och Sedher, wijdskiepellsser, sampt in manga Stycken Grofwe wildfarellsser," in *Berättelser om samerna i 1600-talets Sverige*, ed. Phebe Fjellström (Kungl: Skytteanska Samfundets Handlingar Nr. 27, 1983), 10—12, 47; Johannis J. Tornæi, *Beskrifning öfwer Tornå och Kemi lappmarker* (Stockholm: Kongl. Finska Boktryckeriet, 1772), 63.

21. Milo Milton Quaife, ed., *The Indian Captivity of O. M. Spencer* (New York: Citadel, 1968), 102, 107; DePeyster to Haldimand, November 3, 1781, in *Michigan Pioneer and Historical Collections*, 40 vols. (Lansing: Pioneer and Historical Society of the State of Michigan), 10:537 (hereafter cited as *MPHC*); William L. McDowell, Jr., ed., *Colonial Records of South Carolina: Documents Relating to Indian Affairs, May 21, 1750—August 7, 1754* (Columbia: South Carolina Archives Department, 1958), 423.

22. Enbuske, *Vanhan Lapin valtamailla*, 70, 76—99, 102—3, 501; Mauno Hiltunen, *Maailma maailmojen välissä: Enontekiön asukkaat, elinkeinot ja maanhallinta, 1550—1808* (Helsinki: Oikeusministeriö, 2006), 63—70.

23. Hiltunen, *Maailma maailmojen välissä*, 65—66, 101; Tinget i Enontekis, Svea Hovrätts arkiv (hereafter cited as SHA), Domböcker för år 1669: Gävleborgs län 1668—1669, vol. 18, National Archives of Sweden, Stockholm (hereafter cited as NAS); Tinget i Enontekis 1674, SHA, Domböcker för år 1673—1674, Gävleborgs län 1673—1674, vol. 22, NAS.

24. Hansen and Olsen, *Samenes historie*, 261—62; Roger Kvist, "Swedish Saami Policy, 1550—1990," in *Readings in Saami History, Culture and Language III*, ed. Roger Kvist (Umeå: University of Umeå, 1992), 63—77; Ritva Kylli, *Saamelaisten kaksi kääntymystä: Uskonnon muuttuminen Utsjoen ja Enontekiön lapinmailla, 1602—1905* (Helsinki: SKS, 2012), 34—94.

25. Prostvisitationsprotokoll, 1770 § 3, 11, Utsjoki kyrkoarkiv PII: 1, Provincial Archives of Oulu (hereafter cited as PAO).

26. K. M:ts svar på Baltzar Becks, June 27, 1608, Riksregistraturet 1608: Kungl Maj:ts kansli, NAS; Tinget i Enontekis, SHA, Domböcker för år 1695: Västerbottens län 1695, vol. 6, NAS; Tinget i Enontekis, SHA, Domböcker för år 1707: Västerbottens län 1706—1707, vol. 12, NAS.

27. Fur, *Colonialism in the Margins*, 62—63, 68; Karin Granqvist, "Confrontation and Conciliation: The Sami, the Crown and the Court in Seventeenth-Century Swedish Lapland," *Acta Borealia* 21, no. 2 (2004): 99—116; Granqvist, *Samerna, staten och rätten*, 12, 20, 146—47; Lars Ivar Hansen, "Trade and Markets in Northern Fenno-Scandinavia, A.D. 1550—1750," *Acta Borealia* 1, no. 2 (1984): 47—79.

28. Kvist, "Nomadic Saami and Alcohol," 187.

29. Fur, *Colonialism in the Margins*, 80; Nicolai Lundii Lappi, "Desciptio Lapponiæ," in *Berättelser om samerna*, ed. Fjellström, 11, 15.

30. Lakomäki, *Gathering Together*, 24—30; Warren, *Worlds the Shawnees Made*, 57—79.

31. Samuel Hazard, ed., *Minutes of the Provincial Council of Pennsylvania*, 16 vols. (Harrisburg, Pa., 1838—1853), 5:350 (hereafter cited as *MPCP*).

32. *MPCP*, 3:21, 49, 97; *MPCP*, 4:347; Proceedings of William Fairfax with

Iroquois Chiefs and Their Allies at Winchester, September 10–17, 1753, in *Virginia Treaties, 1723–1775*, ed. W. Stitt Robinson (Frederick, Md.: University Publications of America, 1983), 182.

33. *MPCP*, 3:463; *MPCP*, 4:344.

34. Gov. Gordon to the Shawanese Indians, 1731, in *Pennsylvania Archives*, eds. Samuel Hazard et al., 9 ser., 138 vols. (Philadelphia, 1852–1949), 1st ser., 1:303 (hereafter cited as *PA*).

35. Mancall, *Deadly Medicine*, 57. For a broader analysis of British understandings of gift-giving, see Gregory Evans Dowd, "'Insidious Friends': Gift Giving and the Cherokee–British Alliance in the Seven Years' War," in *Contact Points: American Frontiers from the Mohawk Valley to the Mississippi, 1750–1830*, eds. Andrew R. L. Cayton and Frederika J. Teute (Chapel Hill: University of North Carolina Press, 1998), 114–50.

36. Proceedings of William Fairfax with Iroquois Chiefs and Their Allies at Winchester, September 10–17, 1753, in *Virginia Treaties*, ed. Robinson, 182.

37. *MPCP*, 9:259 (quotation).

38. Speech of the Makujays to the King, William Claus Papers (MG 19), 7:126, reel C-1479, Library and Archives Canada, Ottawa (hereafter cited as LAC) (quotations); Speech of the Shawanoe Prophet and Shawawnoe King, [November 1814?], Indian Affairs (RG 10), 29:17520, reel C-11008, LAC.

39. Speech of the Makujays to the King, William Claus Papers (MG 19), 7:126, reel C-1479, LAC; DePeyster to Haldimand, November 3, 1781, in *MPHC*, 10:537.

40. *MPCP*, 9:261 (quotation); Gregory Evans Dowd, *War under Heaven: Pontiac, the Indian Nations, and the British Empire* (Baltimore: Johns Hopkins University Press, 2002).

41. *Prästeståndets riksdagsprotokoll 4: 1680–1714* (Uppsala: Lennart Thanner, 1962), 230; Ilkka Mäntylä, *Suomalaisen juoppouden juuret: Viinanpoltto vapaudenaikana* (Helsinki: SKS, 1985), 18.

42. Kustaa H. J. Vilkuna, *Juomareiden valtakunta, 1500–1850: Suomalaisten känni ja kulttuuri* (Helsinki: Teos, 2015), 42–43.

43. Mäntylä, *Suomalaisen juoppouden juuret*, 45, 66–67, 81–82, 102–3.

44. Vilkuna, *Juomareiden valtakunta*, 33–59.

45. Fur, *Colonialism in the Margins*, 77.

46. Kongl. Majts förordning, October 3, 1723, Direktionens över Lappmarkens ecklesiastikverk arkiv: Kongl. Majsts Bref m.m., 1680–1742, NAS.

47. Kvist, "Myten om samerna," 3–4; Ritva Kylli, *Kirkon ja saamelaisten kohtaaminen Utsjoella ja Inarissa, 1742–1886* (Rovaniemi: Pohjois-Suomen historiallinen yhdistys, 2005), 282.

48. Tinget i Utsjoki, 1733 § 1, SHA, Domböcker för Norrbottens län 1733, vol. 15, NAS.

49. Kvist, "Myten om samerna," 3–4.

50. Hansen and Olsen, *Samenes historie*, 262–70.

51. For Swedish fears of "losing" the Sámis, see Lennart Lundmark, *Stulet land: Svensk makt på samisk mark* (Stockholm: Ordfront, 2008), 23, 50.

52. Kvist, "Samerna och alkoholen," 123.

53. Första Bihang eller Codecill till Gränsse Tractaten emellan Konunga

Rikerne Swerige och Norge, Lappmännerne beträffade, *Studier i renbeteslag-stiftning,* eds. Tomas Cramér and Gunnar Prawitz (Stockholm: Norstedt, 1970), 108–15.

54. Henric Wegelii berättelse, April 7, 1763, Direktionens över Lappmarkens ecklesiastikverk arkiv: Handlingar, 1763–1767, NAS; Hansen and Olsen, *Samenes historie,* 276.

55. *MPCP,* 2:257.

56. Indians at Allegheney to Gov., March 20, 1738, in *PA,* 1st ser., 1:551.

57. Extract from a Talk from Melonthy to John Wyllys, June 8, 1786, in *Revolution and Confederation,* ed. Colin G. Calloway (Bethesda, Md.: University Publications of America, 1994), 355 (quotation); Lakomäki, *Gathering Together,* 35–36.

58. *MPCP,* 2:29, 43, 257; Indians' Letter to Gov. Gordon, 1733, in *PA,* 1st ser., 1:394.

59. Mancall, *Deadly Medicine,* 28, 121–28.

60. *MPCP,* 3:129 ("Country . . ."); *MPCP,* 4:740 ("carry'd . . .").

61. *MPCP,* 3:365.

62. Indian Letter Respecting Indian Traders, in *PA,* 1st ser., 1:425; Indians at Allegheney to Gov., March 20, 1738, ibid., 551 (quotations).

63. Lakomäki, *Gathering Together,* 42–55.

64. An Indian Conference, November 12, 1768, in *The Papers of Sir William Johnson,* ed. James Sullivan et al., 14 vols. (Albany: State University of New York Press, 1921–1965), 12:635; Johnston to the Editors of Liberty Hall, August 27, 1811, Shawnee File, Ohio Valley–Great Lakes Ethnohistory Archive, Indiana University, Bloomington.

65. Colin G. Calloway, *The Scratch of a Pen: 1763 and the Transformation of America* (Oxford, U.K.: Oxford University Press, 2006), 92–98; Dowd, *War under Heaven,* 177–78.

66. Plan for the Imperial Control of Indian Affairs, July 10, 1764, in *Collections of the Illinois State Historical Library, Vol. 10: The Critical Period, 1763–1765,* eds. Clarence Walworth Alford and Edwin Carter (Springfield: Trustees of the Illinois Historical Library, 1915), 273; Johnson on the Organization of the Indian Department, in ibid., 334–35 (quotations from 334).

67. Douglas A. Irwin, *Against the Tide: An Intellectual History of Free Trade* (Princeton, N.J.: Princeton University Press, 1996), 24, 32–34.

68. L. C. Green, "Claims to Territory," in *The Law of Nations and the New World,* eds. L. C. Green and Olive P. Dickason (Edmonton: University Press of Alberta, 1989), 1–139 (information from pages 71–74).

69. Ishii, "Alcohol and Politics in the Cherokee Nation," 673–74.

70. Mancall, *Deadly Medicine,* 16, 20 ("art . . ."); *MPCP,* 2:633 ("beasts").

71. Isak Fellman, ed., *Handlingar och uppsatser angående finska lappmarken och lapparne, Vol. I* (Helsingfors: Finska Litteratursällskapets tryckeri, 1910), 467 ("mad"); Pehr Högström, *Befskrifning öfwer de til Sweriges Krona lydande Lappmarker År 1747* (Stockholm: Lars Slavii, 1747), 127 ("crazy").

72. Högström, *Befskrifning,* 127 ("such . . ."); *MPCP,* 8:470 ("Indians . . .").

73. Lewis Cass, "Policy and Practice of the United States and Great Britain in Their Treatment of Indians," *North American Review* 24, no. 55 (1827): 365–442

("excessive . . ." and "individual . . ." from 404, "passion" from 406); E. D. Clarke, *Travels in Various Countries of Scandinavia Including Denmark, Sweden, Norway, Lapland, and Finland,* 2 vols. (London: T. Cadell and W. Davies, 1838), 1: 403 ("love"); Kvist, "Myten om samerna," 9.

74. Reginald Horsman, *Race and Manifest Destiny: The Origins of American Racial Anglo-Saxonism* (Cambridge, Mass.: Harvard University Press, 1981), 4—6; Bruce Nelson, *Irish Nationalists and the Making of the Irish Race* (Princeton, N.J.: Princeton University Press, 2012).

75. "Kirjotus Lapinmaalta," *Turun Wiikkosanomat,* April 7, 1821.

76. Cummins to Harris, September 30, 1836, RG 75: Letters Received by the Office of Indian Affairs, 1824—1881, M234, roll 300, f. 1007, U.S. National Archives, Washington, D.C. (hereafter cited as USNA) ("drinking . . ."); Cummins to Herring, April 9, 1833, ibid., f. 465 ("would . . .").

77. William E. Unrau, *The Rise and Fall of Indian Country, 1825—1855* (Lawrence: University Press of Kansas, 2007).

78. Isaac McCoy, *History of Baptist Indian Missions* (Washington, D.C.: William M. Morrison, 1840), 124 ("wasting . . ."), 265, 322, 327; Exchange of Lands with the Indians, January 9, 1817, in *American State Papers: Documents, Legislative and Executive, of the Congress of the United States,* Class II, *Indian Affairs,* vol. 2, eds. Walter Lowrie and Walter S. Franklin (Washington, D.C.: Gales and Seaton, 1834), 124 ("depraved"); Unrau, *White Man's Wicked Water,* 26.

79. Anderson, *Ethnic Cleansing and the Indian,* 171; Lakomäki, *Gathering Together,* 193.

80. Unrau, *White Man's Wicked Water,* 37—38, 46.

81. *Samling af Placater, Förordningar, Manifester och Påbud,* 321.

82. Kvist, "Nomadic Saami and Alcohol," 188.

83. William E. Unrau, *Indians, Alcohol, and the Roads to Taos and Santa Fe* (Lawrence: University Press of Kansas, 2013), 26—28, 72—74; Unrau, *White Man's Wicked Water,* 30—31, 45—46, 56.

84. Cummins to Harvey, September 26, 1848, RG 75, M234, roll 302, f. 1107—8, USNA ("spirit . . ."); Johnson to Cummins, September 2, 1833, RG 75, M234, roll 300, f. 475, USNA ("show . . .").

85. Warren, *Shawnees and Their Neighbors,* chapter 5.

86. For example, George Minot, ed., *Statutes at Large of the United States of America: From December 1, 1845, to March 3, 1851* (Boston: Little, Brown and Company, 1862), 203.

87. Cummins to Herring, April 9, 1833, RG 75, M234, roll 300, f. 465, USNA.

88. Lakomäki, *Gathering Together,* 212.

89. Henry Harvey, *History of the Shawnee Indians, from the Year 1681 to 1854, Inclusive* (Millwood, N.Y.: Kraus Reprint, 1977), 281—88.

90. Manypenny to Cumming, December 12, 1854, RG 75, M234, roll 364, f. 982, USNA; Bond of C. Chouteau, June 30, 1855, RG 75, M234, roll 809, f. 23, USNA.

91. Prostvisitationsprotokoll, January 1, 1793, Kemin rovastikunnan arkisto, Cd: 1, PAO; Grape till domkapitlet, June 22 1796 § 4, Härnösands domkapitels arkiv FIII: 41, Regional Archives in Härnösand.

92. Kvist, "Nomadic Saami and Alcohol," 192.

93. Lars Hætta and Anders Bær, *Usko ja elämä: Koutokeinon saamelaisten hengellisestä elämästä, Lars Levi Laestadiuksen heräyksestä ja lestadiolaisuuden alkuvaiheista ennen vuotta 1852* (Utsjoki: Girjegiisá Oy, 1993); Neil Kent, *The Sámi Peoples of the North: A Social and Cultural History* (London: C. Hurst & Co., 2014), 110–11; Saarnakopiokirja, Rouva Olga Palton kokoelma, Ba: 1, Laestadiana 12, PAO (quotation).

94. For an overview of the numerous interpretations of this event, see Tapio Nykänen, "Vapaustaistelijoita ja hurmahenkiä: Koutokeinon kapinan tulkintojen historiaa," *Historiallinen Aikakauskirja* 108, no. 4 (2010): 438–50.

95. Sköld and Kvist, "Alkoholen och de nomadiserande samerna," 252; Kvist, "Myten om samerna," 8.

96. Kertomus Lapinmaan kirkkojen ja koulujen tilasta, October 9, 1833, 19/342, Senaatin talousosaston arkisto, Ea929, National Archives of Finland.

97. Brev till kronofogden, October 26, 1863, Utsjoen piirin nimismies, DIA 1:1, Kirjekonseptit 1839–1881, PAO.

98. *Samling af Plakater, Förordningar, Manifester och Påbud, Vol. 17: 1858–1859* (Helsingfors: Kejserliga Senatens för Finland tryckeri, 1862), 588–89; Sköld and Kvist, "Alkoholen och de nomadiserande samerna," 249–50.

99. Greer, "Dispossession in a Commercial Idiom," 86 (quotation). For a broader look at the contested and often contradictory history of the category "Indigenous peoples," see Francesca Merlan, "Indigeneity: Global and Local," *Current Anthropology* 50, no. 3 (2009): 303–33.

KELLY WISECUP

Practicing Sovereignty:
Colonial Temporalities, Cherokee Justice,
and the "Socrates" Writings of John Ridge

BETWEEN 1828 AND 1830, a Cherokee writer using the pseudonym Socrates penned four articles for the *Cherokee Phoenix*. Three pieces appeared in 1828, just after Elias Boudinot began editing and publishing the Cherokee- and English-language newspaper. In a two-part commentary on Georgia's claims to Cherokee land published in late February and early March 1828, Socrates debunked the state's arguments by inserting quotations from books by the Swiss legal theorist Emmerich de Vattel and the colonial historian and minister Alexander Hewatt. In these articles, the pseudonymous writer provides evidence that the Cherokees had long maintained the "right of sovereignty over [their] country" and critiques Georgia's arguments that the Cherokees were savages who could not possess land.[1] Later in 1828, in a third article, titled "Intermarriage," Socrates proposes that the Cherokee Nation establish a central office to monitor marriages between white men and Cherokee women. Socrates's final article was published in July 1830, a few months after Congress passed the Indian Removal Act and soon after the state of Georgia passed laws extending state jurisdiction over Cherokee people, events that had one culmination in the Cherokee challenge to these policies in *Cherokee Nation v. Georgia* in 1831. In this final article, Socrates commented on letters from the War Department regarding the Indian Removal Act, noting that President Andrew Jackson's policies violated treaties and acts of Congress that defined the relationship between Native nations and the United States. Socrates ends this article by envisioning that the Cherokee Nation will outlast this latest attack on their lands, writing, "I believe the people will endure a seige [*sic*] of all this persecution, and continue to call on Congress for help."[2]

Scholars have speculated about Socrates's identity for many years but without conclusive results.[3] However, archival evidence makes possible an identification of the writer behind the pseudonym. A manuscript version of Socrates's two-part 1828 article titled "Strictures on the 'Report of the Joint Committee on the State of the Republic' in the Legislature of Georgia, on the subject of the Cherokee Lands" is held in the John Howard Payne Papers, at the Newberry Library. It is in the handwriting of and is identified as being

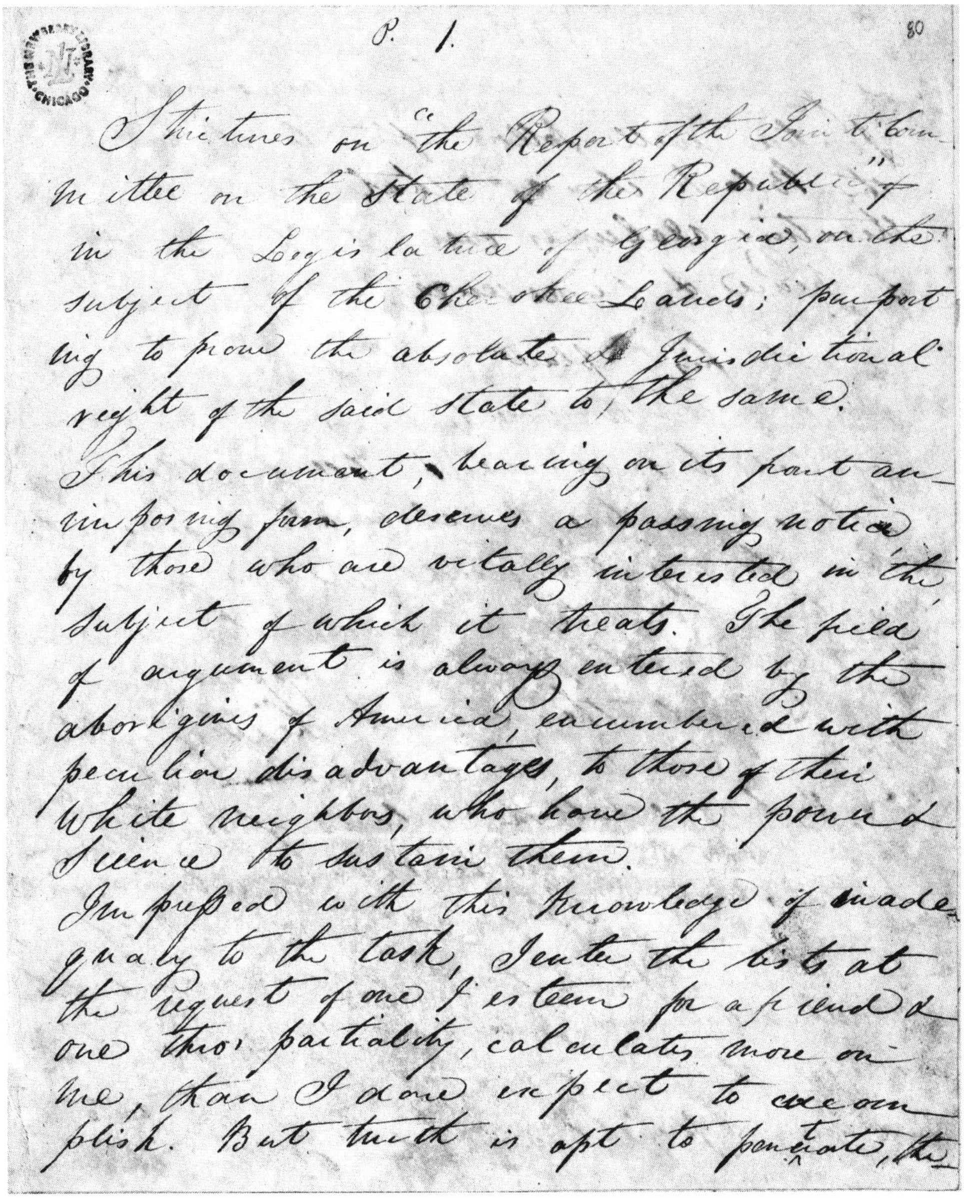

P. 1.   80

Strictures on "the Report of the Joint Committee on the State of the Republic"
in the Legislature of Georgia, on the
subject of the Cherokee Lands; purport-
ing to prove the absolute & Jurisdictional
right of the said state to the same.
This document, bearing on its front an
imposing form, deserves a passing notice
by those who are vitally interested in the
subject of which it treats. The field
of argument is always entered by the
aborigines of America, encumbered with
peculiar disadvantages, to those of their
White neighbors, who have the power &
Science to sustain them.
Impressed with this knowledge of inade-
quacy to the task, I enter the lists at
the request of one I esteem for a friend &
one whose partiality, calculates more on
me, than I dare expect to accom-
plish. But truth is apt to penetrate the

FIGURE 1. "Strictures on the 'Report of the Joint Committee on the State of the Republic' in the Legislature of Georgia, on the Subject of the Cherokee Lands." Photo Courtesy of the Newberry Library, Chicago. Call # Ayer MS 689.

written by John Ridge, the son of Major Ridge, a wealthy Cherokee plantation owner who was also an influential Cherokee leader in the late eighteenth and early nineteenth century, both before and after the Cherokees adopted a constitution and tripartite system of government.[4]

Both Ridges joined a relatively small group of Cherokees who, in the late eighteenth century, adopted Western agricultural practices, religious beliefs, and, in some cases, language and education in response to pressures from the United States.[5] John Ridge, for example, was educated at Brainerd Mission School, run by Moravian missionaries in the Cherokee Nation, and at Cornwall Mission School in Connecticut, where he met his wife, a white Connecticut woman named Sarah Northrup. In the 1820s and 1830s, he served as an amanuensis and spokesman for the Cherokees, giving lectures on Cherokee rights throughout the East Coast, often appearing with his cousin Elias Boudinot or other Cherokee young men.[6] In 1830, Ridge was elected to the Cherokee National Committee. Shortly thereafter, President Jackson refused to require Georgia to defer to federal authority in its dealings with the Cherokee Nation and thus to uphold the Supreme Court's decision in *Worcester v. Georgia* (1832) that Indian policy was under federal jurisdiction. Following these events, the Ridges, Boudinot, and other Cherokees came to the decision that the Nation could best escape threats to its autonomy from states like Georgia by removing to Indian Territory. The Treaty Party, as they came to be called, negotiated with the United States for land in Indian Territory in an attempt to protect Cherokee people from the violence and theft to which Georgians were regularly subjecting them and from which the federal government refused to offer protection. For their decision to sell Cherokee land without the approval of the Cherokees' representative government, a capital offense, the Ridges and Boudinot were executed in 1839.[7]

The connection between Ridge's manuscript version of *Strictures* and its publication under the pseudonym Socrates allows us to attribute the two additional articles to Ridge, thus identifying him as the author of "Intermarriage," and of the 1830 response to the "scrap of extracts" from the War Department.[8] While it is possible that multiple writers for the *Phoenix* adopted the pseudonym Socrates, the Socrates articles are similar in style and subject matter: they compile and critique documents threatening the Cherokees' claims to their lands and their autonomy, systematically illuminating these documents' failures of logic or illegality. Other pseudonymous writers for the *Phoenix* are likewise each characterized by a unique voice and topic, suggesting that the writers linked their pseudonyms with specific tones and themes. For example, writers who contributed to the *Phoenix* under the names "A Cherokee," "A Cherokee Farmer," "A Friend," and "Publius" each took up particular issues: contributions from "A Cherokee" focus on internal politics, while "A Cherokee Farmer" writes primarily about removal. Ridge, like the other pseudonymous writers for the *Phoenix,* adopted a voice that was unique and recognizable for his Socrates articles.[9]

This article shows that Ridge's Socrates articles provided a public venue in which to define relationships among the Cherokees, the states, and the federal government. Ridge's pseudonym facilitated a rhetorical structure that created not only a public persona recognizable to the *Phoenix*'s multiple readerships but also a public character who argued forcefully that white readers should respect Cherokee rights and claims. This persona allowed Socrates to experiment with how to represent sovereignty in a period that fell after the 1823 Supreme Court decision *Johnson v. M'Intosh* limited Native rights to land as that of "occupancy" but before the Court's 1831 decision in *Cherokee Nation v. Georgia,* which defined the Cherokees—and, by extension, Native political entities—as domestic dependent nations. In 1828, Socrates responds to recent attempts to limit Cherokee jurisdiction and governance by turning to the colonial archive. He disassembles Western legal and historical documents in order to lead readers to find their illegalities and to create space in which what he calls "justice" can be enacted.

To do so, Socrates employs literary strategies of compilation in which he collects textual excerpts from Western sources, reassembles them in his articles, and reinterprets their meanings. Socrates does not merely reiterate these sources' arguments, for compilation functions as a key literary and political strategy that transforms what might seem to be imitation into a careful reading of these sources for Cherokee purposes. Compiling these excerpts in new contexts requires that readers participate in the process of reinterpreting them, eventually coming to their own understandings of Cherokee sovereignty as they engage with the text. Importantly, compilation allows Socrates to revise the timeline for the end of Cherokee sovereignty as imagined by the United States: he places previously circulated legal documents such as treaties and U.S. law alongside his commentary on recent events, in this way putting the two in conversation and insisting on the continuing relevance of past treaties and constitutional acts in the present. This methodology creates a space in which past, present, and future Cherokee political relations can exist, against federal and state expectations of vanishing tribal sovereignty and peoples. It also, at times, results in recommendations that differentially affect various people in the Nation, and I trace Ridge's process of articulating sovereignty before examining some of the repercussions of undertaking this process in the context of a settler-colonial state. Ridge's pseudonymous writings offer a unique look into how some Cherokees imagined sovereignty at a moment of transition in both U.S. Indian policy and Cherokee governance.

Socrates's writings also offer the opportunity to reconsider Ridge's place in Native American literary history. While he is well-known as a key figure in nineteenth-century Cherokee politics and history, Ridge has received less attention as a writer. This oversight likely stems from Ridge's use of a pseudonym for some of his printed writings and from the fact that his manuscript writings—including letters to politicians like Albert Gallatin; word lists; translations; and accounts of Cherokee and other southeastern Native peoples—were not published until the twentieth century and, in most cases, remain buried in manuscript collections. Scholars often reference Ridge in studies of Cherokee writings of the period before going on to analyze Elias Boudinot's larger printed archive. If they do analyze Ridge's writings, they focus primarily on his 1826 letter to Gallatin, first printed in 1981, reading it in the context of Ridge's later support for the Treaty Party, in order to argue that he rejected Cherokee practices in favor of Western ones.[10]

Yet when Socrates's writings are considered in the context of U.S. and Cherokee conceptions of sovereignty in the late eighteenth and early nineteenth centuries, they offer a fascinating look at the strategies that Ridge—likely in coordination with Boudinot and Principal Chief John Ross—employed to articulate Cherokee sovereignty, its meanings, and its engagements with U.S. settler-colonialism before Native nations were defined as "domestic dependent nations" and the "wards" of their federal "guardians."[11] His articles illuminate the complicated, unpredictable process of articulating and enacting sovereignty, a process whose outcomes, as Robert Warrior has observed, are undetermined and may be ambivalent.[12] Socrates's writing show the range of expressions that sovereignty could take in the nineteenth-century Cherokee Nation, and they urge us, as his contemporary readers, to attend to those expressions even when they lead to ends that seem to contradict his focus on justice or are at odds with contemporary understandings of sovereignty.

Finally, then, Socrates's work can provide a model with which scholars in multiple disciplines can account for sovereignty as a process, one with undetermined consequences. Warrior's term "intellectual sovereignty" and Scott Richard Lyons's term "rhetorical sovereignty" have become key terms for scholars trained in both Native American and Indigenous studies and in early American literary studies.[13] Native American and Indigenous studies scholars take these terms as foundations for studying sovereignty in contexts constrained by colonialism; similarly, early Americanists have drawn on the terms to illuminate Native Americans' rhetorical and aesthetic choices, even in moments that seem overdetermined by colonialist desires. Yet scholars from the two disciplines position these terms differently: many Native American and Indigenous studies scholars rely on rhetorical or intellectual sovereignty to create an introductory framework through which to define certain actions or writings as expressions of sovereignty. By contrast, early

Americanists tend to use the terms as an endpoint for analysis, a means of retrospectively designating writing as an expression of sovereignty. These methodologies each position choices described as exhibiting rhetorical or intellectual sovereignty by definition as a useful response to colonialism, moves that can foreclose an investigation of the various ways in which sovereignty is practiced and of its complicated repercussions. Reading Socrates's writings as experiments in practicing sovereignty illuminates how engaging with the violence of colonialism can result in seemingly contradictory arguments about sovereignty. Likewise, by considering Socrates's writings in the context of Ridge's subsequent decision to sign the Treaty of New Echota, this article highlights the importance of accounting for the entirety of Warrior's and Lyons's arguments.

Pseudonyms, Socratic "Disputation," and the Cherokee Public Sphere

Recent Cherokee history as well as ancient Western traditions and contemporaneous writings about Socrates likely inspired Ridge to take up his particular pseudonym for the arguments he aimed to make in his *Phoenix* contributions. His education in mission schools and his frequent travels along the East Coast would have exposed him to U.S. conceptions of the Greek philosopher useful in formulating his persona. He first references Socrates in November 1822, in a speech given at the Circular Church in Charleston, South Carolina. On his way home from the Foreign Mission School in Cornwall, Connecticut, to recover from a chronic hip condition, Ridge stopped at the church to urge its congregants to offer financial support for missions to Native nations. Speaking to a large crowd, Ridge argues that Native nations' "safety" from "final extermination" depended on the "exertions of the benevolent."[14] He concludes by imagining that Native children educated at mission schools will go on to illustrious careers, despite the public's failure to imagine such lofty outcomes: "They little think, that the youth they support, may display the patriotism of an Alfred, the wisdom of Socrates, or the legislative talents of a Lycurgus!"[15] This reference to Socrates's wisdom aligns with late eighteenth- and early nineteenth-century U.S. representations of Socrates as a wise philosopher who employed questions to illuminate what his audience did not know and to lead them to greater knowledge. For Ridge, playing the role of a wise man who led unknowing people to greater knowledge may have resonated with his self-fashioning as someone who possessed intellectual tools that some of his fellow Cherokees, especially those who had not received a Western education, did not.

In the 1820s and 1830s, the "Socratic method" as we understand it today was not an established pedagogical method, but well-known and widely published discussions of the mind, logic, language, and history frequently referred to Socrates or the "Socratic way of disputation" to describe a mode of learning through discussion and dialogue, a method utilized in multiple contexts.[16] In an 1819 American edition of his book on logic and education, *The Improvement of the Mind,* Isaac Watts noted that the method of "writing controversies by questions only" could make answers to these questions "so plain and so necessary that they are not expressed, because the query itself carries a convincing argument in it and seems to determine what the answer must be."[17] He recommended presenting Christian catechisms as a "Socratical dispute by question and answer" to improve children's powers of reasoning even while also providing religious instruction.[18] Similarly, in his multivolume work *The Origin and Progress of Language,* a book that many U.S. politicians and men of science consulted in their studies of Native American languages, James Burnet, Lord Monboddo noted the possibilities and dangers of what he called the "way of Socratic dialogue, such as we have in Plato and Xenophon, where a man, by proper interrogatories, is made to convict himself of ignorance and vanity."[19] As Monboddo explained, "But, though it be the most effectual of all methods of conviction when it is at all practicable, it is the most unpleasant, and the very attempting it, if we should not succeed, gives the greatest offence. Nor do I wonder, that Socrates, by practicing it, drew such an odium upon himself from the Athenians, as, I am persuaded, was the cause of his death, not the accusation of impiety, and corrupting the youth; for neither which, it does not appear, there was the least ground."[20] Leading an interlocutor to knowledge by first bringing him to admit his own "ignorance and vanity" was a very effective method but also one that held the potential to anger one's audience, sometimes even dangerously.

In addition to encountering descriptions of Socrates in philosophical writings, Ridge and Boudinot would also have encountered references to him in northern and southern newspapers. Indeed, the press may be the most relevant context for Ridge's decision to take on the pseudonym, given the frequency with which the philosopher is referenced in newspapers in the early nineteenth century, as well as editors' habit of republishing articles from various newspapers, a practice in which Boudinot also engaged.[21] Rather than citing specific sources—whether Watts, Monboddo, or the Greek philosophers such as Plato through whom people accessed Socrates's teachings—these newspapers created a public, popular understanding of the philosopher as a man who stood—and died—for certain values. Newspapers printed aphorisms attributed to Socrates, identifying him with wisdom, morality, and love of country and of democracy. Many articles cite—without providing historical context—Socrates's role as a voice for morality and against tyranny, his critique of the Greek government, and his death for his unwelcome criticism. His reputation for critiquing tyranny was especially prescient for the relatively new United States, and articles assured readers that their "representative republic" would, unlike Greece's "pure democracy," protect against "powerful and sudden excitement" from the people, which might lead to poor decisions like the one to execute Socrates.[22] This aspect of Socrates's reputation seems to have been appealing to Ridge, for the *Phoenix*'s Socrates presents himself as a man standing against the tyranny of Georgia and of the United States, especially against their failures to respect the treaties and laws governing their relations with the Cherokee Nation. However, Ridge and other Cherokees would not have been so confident that the "representative republic" of the United States would protect that nation from making poor decisions that held grave consequences for Cherokee people. Moreover, Ridge's decision to assume the pseudonym of a man killed by his own people may have hinted at a prescient sense of his own fate.

When Ridge took on the pseudonym "Socrates," then, he was aligning himself with a figure known for wisdom and for challenging readers to accept hard truths and to see ideas they imagined as uncontroversial through a different lens. At the same time, Ridge's Socrates writings place him in a literary tradition of Native writers who used pseudonyms to critique state and federal policies and officials and to argue for Indigenous sovereignty. For example, the Creek newspaper writer and poet Alexander Posey and the Cherokee writer Dewitt Clinton Duncan created literary personae, Fus Fixico and Too-qua-stee, respectively, in Indian Territory in the 1870s and 1880s. Through these personae, they critique, parody, and debate political issues involving relations among their nations, the United States, and the nascent state of Oklahoma. Duncan and Posey employed humor, satire, and characteristics unique to their personae to critique state and federal attempts to usurp control of Cherokee and Creek land, respectively, and to argue for the ongoing importance of separate Native political structures. As Craig Womack has shown in his reading of the Fus Fixico letters, Posey did not replicate Western humorists in his adoption of a pseudonym and use of satire; instead, he relied on Creek oral histories, incorporating details from those stories to critique both Creek and U.S. leaders.[23] Similarly, as I show below, Ridge took up the name Socrates and engaged with Western texts in order to relay Cherokee interpretations of treaties, of sovereignty, and of their relation to place. Placing Ridge in this literary history thus also positions his Socrates writings as an early moment in an Indigenous literary history of pseudonymous critique and satire, employed to point out the faults of powerful people and political entities.

Given his arguments about Cherokee rights to their land and about state and federal responsibilities to uphold past agreements, Socrates's writings are most likely aimed at a white readership who might imagine that Georgia's claims to land superseded Cherokee ones or who considered supporting removal. Moreover, Ridge utilized his pseudonym to build the *Phoenix*'s readership, especially in the Northeast, where many white readers sympathetic to the Cherokees' cause subscribed to the paper. In this respect, the *Phoenix*'s pseudonymous publication practices aligned with broader, eighteenth- and nineteenth-century methods of print publication and circulation, especially those adopted by small, local newspapers. Ridge and other Cherokee writers seem to have approached the challenge of developing a readership much as their Anglo-American peers had: by experimentally "assuming masks" that they hoped would become a noteworthy and desirable aspect of the paper.[24] The *Phoenix,* like many other papers, was produced by a small team, with Boudinot acting as both printer and editor, aided by an apprentice, and with input from Ross and other leaders. The paper circulated throughout the Northeast through personal networks in urban centers and missionary circles. Given the importance of these personal contacts to the paper's circulation, it is likely that multiple people, within and outside the Cherokee Nation, were aware of—and enjoyed knowing—Socrates's identity. Moreover, by 1828, Ridge already had a reputation as a speaker on Cherokee rights, and the knowledge that it was Ridge writing as Socrates may have drawn readers to his *Phoenix* articles.[25]

As Phillip H. Round has pointed out, the *Phoenix*'s letters to the editor allowed Cherokees to "'sign on' to the public sphere the paper had constructed by allowing their signatures and pseudonyms to stand as markers of self-fashioning."[26] Eighteenth- and nineteenth-century writers for newspapers often adopted a variety of pseudonyms that suggested "salable identities, personae through which to speak. If one name caught on, one kept it as a durable resource."[27] Such self-fashioning was not only an exercise in creativity but also a political tactic Ridge employed to urge Georgia and the United States to honor Cherokee rights to their lands, as well as their own existing laws. "Socrates" allowed Ridge to fashion Cherokee identities and jurisdiction in ways useful to the project of protecting his homelands but not necessarily coextensive with internal understandings of the "right of sovereignty," just as Socrates the character was related to but not necessarily coextensive with John Ridge the man.[28] Moreover, the pseudonym may have offered some protection from criticism: Ridge's public speeches and writings highlight the embodied and potentially dangerous nature of appearing in public to argue for Cherokee rights. For example, in an April 1831 letter against removal, Ridge notes that the newspapers, politicians, and leaders who "throw clouds and darkness upon our rights" make the "voice of an Indian . . . feeble."[29] This description highlighted the difficulty of contributing to a public sphere already circulating stereotypical and racist images of Native peoples. He notes in "Strictures" that the "aborigine" enters the "field of argument . . . encumbered with peculiar disadvantages."[30] In the context of these disadvantages, "Socrates" offers a character through whom Ridge could adopt a position of knowledge, raise challenging questions, and lead his potentially skeptical audience to new knowledge by guiding them through answers to those questions.

The pseudonym thus did not create an anonymous—and by extension, disinterested and objective—position from which to critique Georgia and the United States, nor was anonymity necessarily desirable for Ridge or other Cherokee writers, for whom the social authentication of messages had long been key to their authority.[31] "Socrates" functioned as a character for Ridge, one he inhabited temporarily in order to question white readers' assumptions about Cherokee sovereignty. Yet Ridge and other writers, like Posey, also used pseudonyms to strengthen Indigenous communities and social ties. Ridge's writing as Socrates invited readers in the know, many of whom would have been in the Cherokee Nation, to participate in the pleasure of reading the allegedly anonymous writing of someone they knew quite well, or of laughing at a thinly disguised parody of their leaders. And, as Womack points out, Posey sought a Creek audience by insisting that his letters about the dangers of Oklahoma statehood be published locally and refusing to seek out an eastern audience.[32] Posey's use of dialect and metaphor allow him to speak in a "code" understood by readers in the know, thus creating a rhetorical space in which "insiders [can] communicate safely."[33] Likewise, Ridge's publication of his Socrates's writings in the *Phoenix* points to his immersion in the Cherokee community of leaders who worked out how to use the newspaper to advocate for Cherokee autonomy and his engagement with a larger Cherokee readership who followed his critiques of Georgia and the United States from the perspective of readers already in the know.

Temporalities of Sovereignty

In addition to Cherokee readers of the *Phoenix,* Socrates addressed white audiences, both those elite whites in the Northeast who strongly opposed Jackson and his policies of Indian removal and those white readers in the Southeast who actively opposed Cherokee sovereignty. The years 1828–1830 constituted a key moment in which to address both audiences. Socrates wrote for the *Phoenix* five years after the Supreme Court's decision in *Johnson v. M'Intosh,* which ruled that Native people did not hold title to their lands that they could convey to white settlers. Instead, Native people had merely the rights of "occupancy."[34] In this case, the Court reinterpreted the Doctrine of Discovery to mean that European discoverers had a "superior claim" to the land they had discovered, rather than simply the right to treat with the Native peoples settled on those lands, as European nations had previously interpreted that doctrine.[35] As David E. Wilkins and K. Tsianina Lomawaima argue, "Marshall's articulation of an expansive doctrine of discovery in *Johnson* allowed that tribes were 'rightful occupants of the soil,' but that their legal claim to their lands was less than—secondary to—the claim of the U.S."[36] *Johnson* thus contradicted existing precedent as well as "statutory law, and sovereign pronouncements pointing to a more accurate understanding that the discovery doctrine merely gave the alleged 'discoverer' the right to be the exclusive purchaser of any land the tribes were willing to sell."[37]

Much of this precedent was established late in the eighteenth century, as the United States worked out how to envision relations between Native tribes and the United States. As Henry Knox, George Washington's secretary of state, noted in letters that helped to establish federal Indian policy, "The Indians being the prior occupants, possess the right of the soil. It cannot be taken from them unless by their free consent, or by the right of conquest in case of a just war. To dispossess them on any other principle, would be a gross violation of the fundamental laws of nature, and of that distributive justice which is the glory of a nation."[38] Knox commented further that while Congress had assumed after the Treaty of Paris ended the American Revolution in 1783 that the United States held title to all Indian lands within its boundaries, Native nations disagreed, and Congress subsequently acted in ways that affirmed Native possession of their land.

In the case of the Cherokees, the Treaties of Hopewell (1785) and of Holston (1791) established Cherokee boundaries as distinct from those of the United States and formed a relationship between the two nations in which they interacted as separate entities. In addition, the Treaty of Holston initiated George Washington's civilization policy among the Cherokees, by including provisions for leading "the Cherokee nation . . . to a greater degree of civilization, and to become herdsmen and cultivators, instead of remaining in a state of hunters," and promising that the "U.S. will from time to time furnish gratuitously the said nation with useful implements of husbandry."[39] As Thomas Jefferson articulated in an 1803 letter to Indiana territorial governor William Henry Harrison, the civilization policy acknowledged Native sovereignty in the present while also anticipating a future moment in which Native nations would, on their own accord, relinquish their lands and assimilate within the political and geographic boundaries of the United States.[40] Similarly, in the same 1789 letter in which he acknowledges Natives' ownership of their own lands, Knox anticipates that expanding white settlement and diminished game will "reduce" the Indians to a "very small number."[41] Knox, Jefferson, and other officials anticipated that promoting agriculture over hunting and adopting trading policies that left Native people in debt would eventually lead to land cessions so that, as Jefferson put it, "In this way our settlements will gradually circumscribe and approach the Indians, and they will in time either incorporate with us as citizens of the U.S., or remove beyond the Mississippi."[42] It was within this framework that Jefferson could promise Georgia that the United States would eventually extinguish Cherokee title to land near the state boundaries, a promise that, in 1828, just before Socrates picked up his pen, the Georgia Committee insisted should guide federal policy regarding the Cherokees.

Thus the early purveyors of the civilization policy imagined Native, and specifically Cherokee, sovereignty as defined by political separateness from the United States and by the possession of land, and they acknowledged that congressional acts and treaties supported the recognition of that status. At the same time, they imagined that this sovereignty was limited by a future moment in which Native nations would no longer exist as separate political entities and were no longer the "only rightful proprietors of the soil."[43] Cherokee sovereignty as the United States envisioned it was a condition that lasted only as long as it took for the Cherokees to become encompassed within the geographic boundaries and populations of the United States, a project the civilization policy was designed to bring about. When Socrates wrote, then, the United States had acknowledged the Cherokees and other Native nations as independent, sovereign people in multiple treaties. The United States had likewise followed Knox's precedent by mandating that the federal government, not states, would negotiate with tribes. Yet the Supreme Court in 1823 had also, as Maureen Konkle points out, "conceded Native autonomy, but in the sense of it being almost momentary, lasting only long enough for Indians to enter into willing treaty agreements with U.S. officials in order to transfer land."[44]

Socrates's articles appeared at a moment when white settlers were illegally encroaching on Cherokee lands in increasing numbers. By this time, the Cherokees had incorporated many of the Western practices required by the Treaty of Holston, an agreement that, as Tiya Miles points out, suggested that U.S. protection from white intruders was contingent on the Cherokees' adoption of Western forms of agriculture, education, and religion.[45] After almost forty years, federal and state officials as well as U.S. settlers began to argue that the anticipated moment of tribes' limited or absent sovereignty had arrived. This claim appears in the Supreme Court decision in *Johnson* that tribes possessed only the right of occupancy to their land; it appears as well in Georgia's insistence in its 1828 *Report* that the Cherokees lacked the right of possession to their lands and that the United States should fulfill its promise to extinguish Cherokee title within what Georgia claimed as its boundaries.[46]

Compilation, Law, and Simultaneity

In his first, paired set of articles, Socrates first acknowledges the ways that the United States shaped and limited Cherokee sovereignty with treaties, legal theories, and Supreme Court cases in order to then critique Georgia's *Report*. Both the content and form of "Strictures" display this enmeshment: in this article, Socrates argues that the Cherokees are legitimate possessors of their lands by turning not only to tribal conceptions of land use or to oral histories about their origins but also to theories of possession and history articulated in Emmerich de Vattel's 1758 *Law of Nations* and Alexander Hewatt's 1779 *An Historical Account of the Rise and Progress of the Colonies of South Carolina*. For example, Socrates argues that "the Cherokee Nation is composed of a number of free families, spread over a District of Country which has been held by them from time immemorial" and that these families have "legal possession" of the land.[47] Here, he grounds his characterization of the Nation by quoting from Vattel's book, namely, his premise that "free families" that "come to unite for the purpose of forming a nation or state, . . . all together acquire the sovereignty over the whole country they inhabit."[48]

Socrates likewise founds the claim that the Cherokees have possessed their lands from "time immemorial" in stories of their origins, which he obtains by excerpting Hewatt's *Historical Account*. He writes, quoting directly from Hewatt:

> From time immemorial they have had possession of the same territory which at present they occupy. They affirm that their forefathers sprung from the ground, or descended from the clouds upon those hills. These lands of their ancestors they value above all things in the world. They venerate the places where their bones lie interred, and esteem disgraceful in the highest degree to relinquish their depositories. The man that would refuse to take the field in defense of their hereditary possessions, is regarded by them as a coward & treated as an outcast from their nation.[49]

By drawing on a colonial source for his account of Cherokee history, Socrates appears to position his thinking on sovereignty squarely within Western traditions, and indeed, one might read Socrates (as scholars have read Ridge) as imagining the Cherokee Nation within the framework of U.S. national discourse, a move that allowed the United States to recognize Cherokee sovereignty on its own terms. His methodology of excerpting, quoting, and compiling European sources to describe Cherokee histories would seem to indicate how, as Mark Rifkin has pointed out, the "U.S. government has superimposed legal identities that seek to constrain and manage the self-representations of domesticated groups, producing the appearance of recognition for them and acquiescence by them."[50]

But Socrates does not read Vattel and Hewatt straightforwardly, for he uses their texts to disassemble and open for critique the Georgia Committee's *Report*. Throughout "Strictures," Socrates stages a series of questions and answers with Vattel about sovereignty and the right to possess land. He answers these questions himself—producing an imaginary Socratic disputation—by excerpting and reprinting Europeans' and Georgians' own words; querying them; and drawing out the legal and logical failures of their defenses for appropriating Native lands. Furthermore, Socrates does not merely reiterate or copy Vattel's and Hewatt's points, and he does not simply select different quotations than the Georgia Committee did in order to create a counterargument that justified Cherokee claims to land. His critique goes beyond merely assembling familiar sources to disagree with Georgian claims to Cherokee land.[51] As he disassembles the *Report* and Vattel's and Hewatt's texts and reassembles them in the *Phoenix,* Socrates transforms those texts by placing them in the context of the Cherokees' history and continuing possession of land.[52]

For example, Socrates excerpts key passages from Vattel in order to critique both his characterization of Native land use and corresponding assumptions about land possession. Vattel explicitly addresses Native Americans' rights to the land by noting in *Law of Nations,* "There is another celebrated question, to which the discovery of the new world has principally given rise. It is asked whether a nation may lawfully take possession of some part of a vast country in which there are none but erratic nations whose scanty population is incapable of occupying the whole?"[53] Vattel concludes that European nations could lawfully possess "part of a vast country" occupied only by "erratic nations," writing that "their unsettled habitation in those immense regions cannot be accounted a true and legal possession; and the people of Europe, too closely pent up at home, finding land of which the savages stood in no particular need, and of which they made no actual and constant use, were lawfully entitled to take possession of it, and settle it with colonies."[54] This argument and others like it laid the foundation for nineteenth-century Supreme Court decisions. For example, John Marshall used similar language to write the majority opinion in *Johnson,* arguing that "Indians'" "character"—their "savage" way of life, namely, their reliance on hunting and their life in the "wilderness"—justified Europeans' exclusive rights to the land (rather than their rights to purchase the land from Native people exclusive of other European nations).[55]

Socrates intervenes in both state and federal conceptions of temporary Native sovereignty by reinterpreting Vattel's text. He writes, "If, then, wandering Indians were not allowed to monopolize such countries, they yet had a right to *their share,* which the sword of the Invader could not lawfully take away."[56] Presenting Vattel's theories while contesting their conclusions, Socrates argues that Cherokee people had no right to empire or domain of all of North America, that is, no right to "monopolize" the entire country. Nonetheless, they did have a "right to their share," to the land they occupied, used, and denominated as theirs. Moreover, colonists' right to possess unsettled lands did not void Cherokees' right to that share. That is, Europeans might claim unoccupied lands in America, but this right did not extend to those lands held and inhabited by Native peoples. Socrates likewise detaches agriculture from possession, by arguing that "wandering Indians" had a right to land, even if European nations did not recognize their mode of subsistence as one that marked the possession of land. He pushes further, by questioning the assumption on which Vattel's argument rests, noting that "there is a question whether the Cherokees could ever have been properly called an erratic nation. Let us look to history for information."[57]

Socrates turns to a pre-contact moment to examine Cherokee political governance, one prior to their adoption of practices that Anglo-Americans deemed civilized and a sign of civil governments. He describes the Cherokees as an empire when European colonization began, writing that "Georgia asserted a claim to a vast extent of country, of itself an Empire, if its extent is considered, then owned and in the possession of formidable and warlike Indians, whose southern frontier bordered on the Spanish Provinces."[58] By defining Cherokee lands as an empire based on its "extent," rather than on the basis of rule by a single leader, Socrates draws on contemporaneous uses of the term to refer to "extensive dominion or sovereignty," which could be held by an emperor or by a sovereign state.[59] Given his citation of eighteenth-century sources in this article, Socrates may also have conceived of "empire" in one of its eighteenth-century uses, which referred to an autonomous nation or country.[60] In each case, his use of "empire" corresponded to the Cherokees' system of autonomous towns that collectively controlled an extensive area of land. This description of an "Empire . . . owned and in the possession" of Native nations suggests the existence of Indigenous modes of governing prior to contact, modes that countered state claims to land and on which the Cherokees could build present and future expressions of their rights.

Socrates then looks "to history for information" by extracting and compiling quotations about Cherokee political organization before and after British colonization. He counters Georgia's assertions of Cherokee savagery by placing Hewatt's account of Cherokee negotiations with British officials against Georgia's *Report.* The Georgia Committee had claimed Cherokee lands by arguing in its *Report* that those lands were formerly under the protection of

Great Britain and then were transferred to the United States and, by extension, to Georgia after the Revolutionary War. Socrates quotes the Committee: "'In the exercise,' say the committee, 'both of domain and empire on the part of Great Britain, certain portions of territory were reserved to the use of the Indians, and the Indians themselves were declared to be under the protection of Great Britain, and the Lands reserved were declared to be under the sovereignty, protection and domain of that Government.'"[61] Socrates draws on the "early history of Georgia" in order "to understand the true state of the subject in regard to the Indians & Georgia." He counters the Committees' assertions with a quotation from Hewatt's account of negotiations between British colonist James Oglethorpe and the Cherokees for land on which to build a colony, writing that "after Oglethorpe represented the power and wealth of Great Britain & the benefits that would arise to the Indians from a connection & friendship with them, he went on to say, 'as they had plenty of Lands, he hoped they would freely resign a share of them to his people who were come among them for their benefit and instruction. After having distributed some presents, which must always attend a proposal of friendship and peace, an agreement was made.'—This cannot be misunderstood."

What "cannot be misunderstood" is that Oglethorpe negotiated for and received only a share of Cherokee lands, not all of them. The Cherokee maintained their own lands and continued to govern on those lands in ways they selected, because no European nations ever settled or possessed those lands. Socrates further concludes that, at the end of the Revolutionary War, Great Britain's title to lands and rights to trade with Native people were not merely transferred to the United States but "forfeited . . . forever."[62] The colonies and, later, the states, could not simply claim rights to Native land, for they had "destroyed their connection with the Mother County." As a result, "the Indians were thrown in their original condition, unencumbered of treaties, capable of fighting and perishing on their lands or of making treaties with those alone who had the power, the U.S." Socrates compiles evidence from the historical record, legal theory, and historical events within the memory of living U.S. settlers, all of which indicate that the Cherokees "were settled in towns over this territory, before a white man ever appeared on these shores, and when he did appear and made discovery, he only discovered the Cherokees in peaceable possession of a country, given them from the Almighty." They can trace their possession of their lands from "time immemorial," and they can provide evidence that they never relinquished their land to Great Britain, to the United States, or Georgia. Socrates turns the Western legal and historical tradition against itself, to show that pro-removal arguments and, by extension, *Johnson v. M'Intosh* are contradicted by the very histories that those individuals and institutions claim as their own.

Compiling quotations from Vattel, Hewatt, and the Georgia *Report* does not reiterate these texts' assumptions but operates as a critical methodology with which Socrates recontextualizes the texts. This methodology requires that we not only analyze his *Phoenix* articles at the level of content and representation but also attend to the articles as material texts, constituted by acts of disassembling, rearranging, and representing Western texts in new contexts. Compilation functions in Socrates's articles as a principle of selection and of relation: he extracts textual fragments from multiple documents and contexts before rearranging them in his article, placing previously disparate quotations into relation with one another and with Cherokee histories. This methodology produces texts with a non-narrative, non-hierarchical structure and, importantly, a non-linear temporality: compilation accumulates, producing thick descriptions and fragments that can be assembled and reassembled into multiple relations, while also allowing various historical moments to be considered simultaneously.[63] Significantly, compilation posits an alternative temporality to the United States' linear and fixed timeline, one in which the Cherokees' past political governance has no ending point but is relevant and powerful in the present.

The new contexts in which Socrates places texts by Vattel, Hewatt, and the Georgia Committee alter their meanings and possible interpretations, thus also opening up new imaginations of Cherokee futures in the southeast. In the same way that Cherokees adopted some Western practices as part of the "civilization policy" and transformed them to meet their own needs, so Socrates incorporated and analyzed European sources to experiment with how to effectively communicate Cherokee sovereignty to *Phoenix* readers. Compilation reimagines sovereignty as the United States defined it, by placing into relation modes of Cherokee governance existing before Europeans arrived; European and Cherokee visions of sovereignty after colonialism; European doctrines of discovery; and Georgia's encroachments. Socrates's *Phoenix* writings are less a capitulation to Western theories of nationhood and sovereignty than a meditation on Western legal theories, their relevance for articulations and enactments of Cherokee sovereignty, and their failures to account for Cherokee forms of "Empire."

As compilation allows Socrates to revise the temporality of U.S. sovereignty, it also requires U.S. readers to rethink present actions and policies involving the Cherokees, a point he reiterates in his final article as Socrates, printed July 10, 1830. While the dominant narrative of the United States held that laws defining Cherokee autonomy and boundaries in the past would not be relevant in the moment of diminished Cherokee sovereignty, Socrates uses compilation to demonstrate that the temporal jurisdiction of laws extends to the present. In his 1830 article, Socrates reports on the "scrap of extracts communicated to the Cherokees by the War Department," a set of documents that presented the "advantages of Cherokee emigration."[64] Socrates takes the "scrap of extracts" as an opportunity to reply to Jackson's arguments for removal and Georgia's 1829 laws claiming jurisdiction over Cherokee lands and individuals. He highlights the illegality of these policies by placing the War Department's scraps alongside the "Intercourse Laws of the United States," a reference to the Trade and Intercourse Acts, a series of acts passed by Congress between 1790 and 1802. When Socrates wrote, the Trade and Intercourse Act of 1802 stood as a more permanent measure than those passed in the 1790s, and it established policies for purchasing Indian lands (requiring that purchase be made by treaty) and for protecting the boundaries of these lands from white expansion, livestock, and crimes. The Act also provides for "domestic animals, and implements of husbandry" to be furnished to "friendly Indian tribes," the materials by which Cherokees' reduced numbers and land base were allegedly to be bought about.[65]

But Socrates refuses to read the civilization policy and the time elapsed since the passage of the Intercourse Laws as evidence for a diminishment of

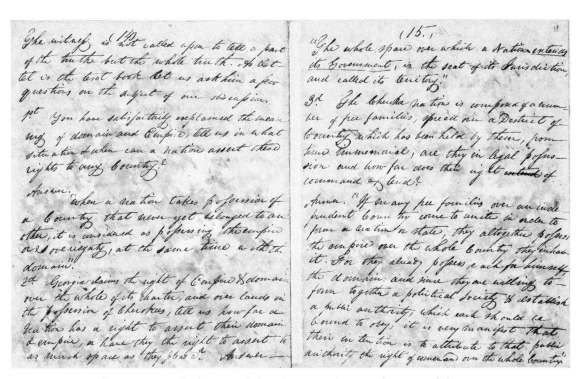

FIGURE 2. "Strictures on the 'Report of the Joint Committee on the State of the Republic' in the Legislature of Georgia, on the Subject of the Cherokee Lands.'" Photo Courtesy of the Newberry Library, Chicago. Call # Ayer MS 689.

Cherokee rights. Instead, he argues that Jackson should consult those laws, the "poor and palsied relic and monument of late Justice and *intercourse of friendship* with this people," and he asks, "Will they not present some obstacles to new, [*sic*] relations?"[66] By placing the War Department's document urging removal and Georgia's recent incursions alongside the "Intercourse Laws," Socrates relies on compilation to present textual "obstacles to new, relations." He uses the space of his article to put legal documents in relation to one another and to present the debates in which those documents engage, thus textually demonstrating how the Trade and Intercourse Act should still govern federal interactions with the Cherokees. The article insists that laws made and acted on in the past still had power, despite U.S. and state arguments that the time had arrived for Cherokee sovereignty over their land and affairs to end.

Similarly, in "Strictures," Socrates envisions the Cherokees' present forms of sovereignty as existing simultaneously with past, precolonial moments, as well as with present and future ones, by looking back to a Cherokee empire and commenting on the present. He writes, "If the Indians were naturally or constitutionally incapable of making treaties, or *contracts*, as some would have it, why was the incompetency not mentioned before and their treaties resisted, and rejected. If any time could be proper, the proper time would have been in their savage state, to have experienced the misfortune rather than now, after tantalizing them, with the hypocritical language of friendship and offers of Civilization and Religion to have their rights and liberties crushed in the cold embrace of Iron power."[67] Socrates puts a number of temporalities into play in this quotation: first, he argues that the time for limiting Cherokee sovereignty has passed, that the assumptions present in treaties between the Cherokees and European or Western nations still stand in the present and are not limited by increasing white populations or Cherokee "civilization." Previously admitting that the Cherokees were autonomous political entities in their "savage state," the United States must now also continue to act in ways that acknowledge this autonomy. By arguing that limiting Native sovereignty is no longer feasible, Socrates also revises narratives that placed Native people out of time and argued that they were not capable of change and would eventually disappear. He shows not only that the Cherokees may no longer be categorized as in a "savage state" but that it is questionable whether they ever were in one: "There is a question whether the Cherokees could ever have been properly called an erratic nation."[68] Socrates highlights the ways that European and U.S. conceptions of "savagery" and "erratic nation[s]" have defined Cherokee sovereignty, but he also insists that these conceptions are inaccurate, that the United States must honor its former recognitions of Cherokee sovereignty and admit that its political categorizations of the Cherokee are inaccurate. In this way, he also suggests that the temporal narratives for framing and limiting Cherokee sovereignty are inadequate and proposes instead a model of simultaneity, enacted in his writings through his compilation of materials and histories from the past and present. The methodology of compilation represents Cherokee jurisdiction in its past, present, and future manifestations. Socrates can thus imagine a future moment when the Cherokees have "endure[d] a siege of all this persecution" and retained their independent status in their homelands.[69] In this context, the Cherokees are capable both of historical change and of maintaining their independent status, one that the United States and Georgia must respect.

Justice and the Settler State

As Socrates redefines U.S. and state visions of limited Cherokee sovereignty, he sometimes refuses to prescribe the forms that Cherokee political and personal relations should take and at other moments offers specific proposals for how people in the United States should change their behavior in light of those relations. In "Strictures," he employs compilation to create space for what he calls "justice," which is enacted by Cherokee people and which requires an admission on the part of Georgia and the United States of the Cherokees' separate and independent status. After rejecting colonial narratives limiting Cherokee sovereignty, Socrates imagines "justice . . . follow[ing] and dispens[ing] the black clouds that hang in threatening volumes over the habitations of peace & innocence."[70] Justice creates space for such "peace & innocence" to emerge among Cherokee "habitations," and it is within this space that Cherokee people can imagine their own forms of governance.[71] The space of justice is both temporal and geographic: justice exists over an area defined by where the Cherokee live: the site of their "habitations." In addition, justice makes possible peace, or political and cultural forms of relating to others in ways that promote collective well-being. Socrates's appeal to justice would also have signaled to white readers that he viewed Cherokee and U.S. sovereignty as based in similar principles, even though Vattel and, following him, Jefferson, Marshall, and other U.S. political leaders argued that these principles did not apply to nations "in their relations to each other."[72] By calling on justice, Socrates argued that all nations were indeed subject to that principle and did not possess what Ian Hunter has called the "sovereign right to determine how best to do this and thence to determine what is just" for each nation.[73] At the same time, Socrates leaves the definition of justice open, refusing to identify it in Western terms and allowing the possibility for Cherokee conceptions of justice to influence how it was enacted. Just as the pseudonym Socrates presented a character attendant to public desires and interest but left open space for a different person to exist beneath the textual character, so the methodology of compilation acknowledges the ways that Cherokee sovereignty is shaped in relation to the United States, but it also leaves space open for the actions that lead to peace and justice, actions that could be embodied and enacted in various ways by Cherokee people. Finally, because justice includes Cherokee governance, it also posits the present as a moment of an autonomy that also existed in the past and will continue to exist in the future.

A few months after the "Strictures" articles were published, Socrates called on white settlers to modify their behavior to account for the space of Cherokee justice. In his May 27, 1828 article, titled "Intermarriages," Socrates advocates creating a central office in which marriages between white men and Cherokee women would be reviewed and approved or disproved, to protect against white men seeking Cherokee land through marriage. Because Cherokee politics and families were matrilineal in nature, Cherokee women's marriages were extremely important, with effects not simply on family structures but also on land ownership and political decisions. Scholars have argued that this article defends Cherokee autonomy at the cost of women's freedom of choice and traditional matrilineal governance.[74] Socrates's argument that a central office, not individual Cherokee women, should make decisions about marriage partners figures in this scholarship as a restriction of Cherokee women's rights and a turn toward viewing Cherokee identity as rooted in "blood" and thus in emerging racial discourses rather than in the clan system. As Fay Yarborough points out, the intermarriage laws passed by the Cherokee Nation in 1819, 1825, and 1827 suggested that Cherokee women could not be trusted to make decisions about their marriages, and they contributed to legal policies restricting the rights and citizenship of women of African descent.[75] As Ann McGrath adds, such racial discrimination allowed the Cherokees to establish governing practices that mirrored those of the United States.[76]

It is true that intermarriage laws restricted women's choices and altered traditional practices of governance. But when this article is read alongside Socrates's body of work and its compilations, the arguments of "Intermarriage" emerge less as a move aimed only at limiting women's choices than as an attempt—if a problematic one—to enact how the forms of sovereignty imagined in "Strictures" might affect U.S. citizens. Socrates's insistence that white men respect Cherokee governance requires a diminishment of U.S. sovereignty. As he writes, "The exercise of sovereignty must necessarily embrace, and touch many, and various objects and interests, but the interests of individuals must sometimes be surrendered and give way to the interest and existence of a nation."[77] While scholars have read this passage as referring to Cherokee women's "interests," Socrates focuses here on the rights of white men who seek to marry into the Nation, individuals who must "surrender" their rights for the "existence of a nation." "Intermarriage" seeks less to limit Cherokee women's rights than to develop the implications of the space of sovereignty and justice imagined in "Strictures" by exploring how it will affect the actions of U.S. men. In this reading, Socrates insists that the United States and its citizens shift their behavior in order to accommodate Cherokee governance, a radical and, for Socrates's readers, perhaps surprising demand in the context of the civilization policy's pressures on Cherokees to assimilate. Socrates makes clear in "Intermarriage" that while Cherokee people might adopt some Western practices, those actions had no bearing on how Cherokees imagined their relation to the United States and their ability to decide what took place on their lands.

Yet because the practice of Cherokee sovereignty occurs within the political and geographic boundaries of the United States, these practices are also subject to being limited and subverted by the competing sovereignty of the U.S. settler state. What might have begun as a proposal to limit white Georgians' actions could be and was transformed into practices that limited Cherokee women's authority and roles. "Intermarriage" thus stands as an example of the ways that settler-colonialism can subvert attempts to articulate and practice sovereignty. As Audra Simpson has pointed out, "In situations in which sovereignties are nested and embedded, one proliferates at the other's expense."[78] These conditions of settler-colonialism and nested sovereignty, as Simpson notes with regard to the Mohawk reserve of Kahnawá:ke, at times forced Indigenous nations to "take an offensive position not just against the settler nation, but in some ways against themselves."[79] Similarly, in the Cherokee Nation, exercising the right to limit white men's actions resulted in procedures and, eventually, laws that also limited and devalued Cherokee women's rights. Socrates's experiments in sovereignty did not always result in "peace and innocence" or in justice; they sometimes enacted sovereignty at the risk of reducing space for Cherokee values and practices, especially those of Cherokee women.[80]

Socrates's writings provide insight into the ways that some members of the Cherokee Nation envisioned their political governance and autonomy at a moment when state and federal governments claimed that the Cherokees merely occupied their land and that the future moment of diminished sovereignty had arrived, but also at a time before the Supreme Court articulated the dependent relationship between Native nations and the United States that has come to dominate federal Indian policy. This moment is one in which Socrates imagines and redefines various models of sovereignty: he makes the Cherokees' past and future autonomy intimately connected to and the foundation for enacting sovereignty in the present. Against U.S. political leaders' arguments that Native nations were limited by a future moment of diminished lands and independence, Socrates posits Cherokee sovereignty as extending into the future, outlasting federal and state pressures to remove. He concludes "Strictures" by stating, "All Nations have their seasons of prosperity and adversity. Mighty empires, that figure with amazing lustre on the page of history, are now silent in awful oblivion."[81] While this statement might now appear to point toward the Cherokee Nation's removal or assimilation, Socrates's point would have been troubling for U.S. readers, who imagined their history as linear and progressive, rather than destined to fade eventually. Throughout his writings, he represents Cherokee sovereignty as limiting the actions of the United States and its people by presenting a history in which the United States will be lost to memory and by insisting that U.S. men abide by Cherokee laws when marrying Cherokee women.

Socrates's methodology highlights the understudied importance of compilation as a textual and material practice for articulating sovereignty in the nineteenth century. Compilation allowed Socrates to represent the ways in which Cherokee sovereignty was entangled with U.S. actions and laws and simultaneously to envision acts of justice taking place in separate political and social spheres. At the same time, compilation highlights the process-oriented nature of sovereignty: its formulation over time and through engagement with multiple sources, through lived actions, and through multiple sets of relations. Yet Socrates's writings also show that practicing sovereignty—and making choices about how the Cherokees were represented—did not always result in justice for all members of the community, especially women and people of African descent, or in the kinds of relations that Socrates imagined with the United States. Instead, supporting sovereignty in the context of settler-colonialism could result in detrimental effects on women's roles and voices. Thus, while "Intermarriage" seeks to limit white men's actions, it also illuminates the gendered costs of arguments for tribal national sovereignty in the nineteenth century and the difficulties Socrates faced as he attempted to create a space for justice that was not exclusive and that did not reiterate Western hierarchies. As the Socrates writings comment on Georgians' depredations, they also make clear the ways in which settler-colonial violence contributed to such exclusions.

"The Justice and Good Faith of the United States"

It does not appear that Ridge wrote as Socrates after his July 10, 1830, article. He continues to write articles that appear in both the *Phoenix* and U.S. newspapers, but he signs his own name to them. This shift seems to have been part of a broader change in tactics and opinion adopted by Ridge, along with

Boudinot and other Cherokees, in response to the Indian Removal Act and to Georgia peoples' increasingly violent and illegal actions, such as squatting on and stealing gold from Cherokee lands and attacking Cherokee property and people. Ridge develops some of Socrates's arguments in his post-1830 writings, arguing in 1831, "Even now, do we believe that if partisan newspapers and leaders, and aspiring politicians, did not throw clouds and darkness upon our rights, that Justice would be continued to our race by the people of the United States."[82] Yet this statement also marks a key change: Ridge focuses on "Justice" as enacted by the United States, shifting his focus from the acts defining justice within the Cherokee Nation to call for the United States to restrain its own citizens. There is also a sense in his post—Removal Act writings that the situation in the Cherokee Nation is increasingly dire, that direct, forceful calls to action are more appropriate than Socratic disputation encouraging U.S. readers to recognize their errors. Ridge may also have decided to write under his own name in order to foreground the reputation he had established in his speeches and his negotiations with the federal government and thus to lend personal authority to these calls to action. Additionally, he likely sought to defend himself in these articles from allegations that he supported removal in order to advance his personal interests. Starting as early as 1830, U.S. newspapers began to circulate reports that Ridge and other Cherokees supported removal and that Ridge, in particular, would seek removal if it would benefit his finances.[83] In the early 1830s, publishing his arguments under his own name was key to dispelling such rumors and to supporting other Cherokees in their resistance to the Removal Act and Georgian depredations.

When President Jackson refused to enforce the Supreme Court decision limiting Georgia's power over the Cherokee Nation in *Worcester v. Georgia* (1832), Ridge, Boudinot, and a minority party of other Cherokees began to consider, and, eventually, to argue, that Cherokee autonomy and safety from federal and state intrusions could be best maintained at a distance from the states. Boudinot's differences with Principal Chief John Ross on this point led him to resign as editor of the *Phoenix* in August 1832, a post later taken up by Elijah Hicks. When the paper began publishing again, Ridge's letters continued to appear in its pages, usually in the form of official reports on debates or decisions in Washington, written in his capacity as a member of the National Committee. These letters sometimes appear alongside notes from the editor stating that Ridge was part of the minority group supporting a treaty that would facilitate removal west.[84]

After 1832, Ridge seems to have become less certain that the arguments he made as Socrates, that the United States should honor its treaties and laws by forcing Georgia to respect Cherokee sovereignty, would be effectual. Writing for the National Committee in the *Phoenix* on November 23, 1833, he noted, "These treaties, laws and the decision of the Supreme Court do not appear to have that moral influence with the President, or the American people which we desire."[85] The decision to write under his own name was thus also part of Ridge's changing understanding of U.S. intentions and his growing, if conflicted, sense that the Cherokees could "determine no other alternative promising relief than a removal beyond the limits of the United States." Even in 1833, Ridge hoped that "this alternative may never present itself, as I cannot for a moment permit myself to entertain so unfavorably opinion [sic] as to loose [sic] all confidence in the justice and good faith of the United States." His eventual loss of confidence in the "justice and good faith" of the United States had one culmination in his signing of the Treaty of New Echota in 1835 and Cherokee removal to Indian Territory.

Questioning and critiquing the "justice and good faith" of the United States remained part of Cherokee processes of articulating and enacting sovereignty after removal. In one iteration of this process, Cherokee writers turned again to pseudonyms and periodical publication to critique "civilization" and legislation such as the Dawes and Curtis Acts. In the early 1880s, Dewitt Clinton Duncan published letters under his pseudonym Too-qua-stee, in which he critiques U.S. policy and its effects on Cherokees in Indian Territory. Born in the Cherokee Nation in 1829, Duncan and his family were forcibly removed with thousands of other Cherokees. Like Ridge, Duncan attended school (Dartmouth College) in the Northeast, and he worked as a teacher and lawyer for the Cherokees starting in 1880. In his letters, published in the *Cherokee Advocate* and *Indian Chieftain,* Too-qua-stee pointedly critiques U.S. policies and white settlers by drawing on strategies similar to those Ridge deploys in the Socrates articles: Too-qua-stee makes historical and biblical references, discusses the history of treaty negotiations, and sharply denounces the difference between U.S. promises and actualities.[86] In 1882, Duncan's "Story of the Cherokees" was published in four installments under his own name. The articles offer a history of Cherokee relations with the state of Georgia that documents the state's greed for land and gold, its citizens' murders of and violence against Cherokee people, and the Supreme Court decisions with monumental consequences for the Cherokees. While Duncan points out that the Cherokees adopted practices deemed civilized, he also notes that they did so in response to colonial greed, a quality he casts as a sickness from which the Cherokees sought to gain "immunity."[87] Moreover, he describes "civilization" as a "malignant power" that "to this day [is] still at their heels demanding their room or their ruin."[88] As Duncan's writing shows, the process of articulating sovereignty in the context of a colonial state continued in Indian Territory, amidst debates about allotment and statehood.

If Ridge hardly resolved this process and even made recommendations and decisions seemingly at odds with justice, his Socrates writings nonetheless provide insight into the range of strategies and forms on which Cherokee writers drew to imagine and practice sovereignty. The Socrates writings are an incomplete and in some cases problematic experiment with sovereignty, but they aim to work out what sovereignty might mean in the world of Cherokee "lived experience" in the nineteenth century.[89] Ridge, like Duncan, Posey, and other writers, employed his writings to imagine a future for Cherokee people, an undetermined and open-ended future, to be sure, but one that outlasted and resisted U.S. colonial designs.

KELLY WISECUP is assistant professor of English at Northwestern University.

Notes

Many thanks to Daniel Heath Justice, an anonymous reader, and Christen Mucher for their comments on this article. Thanks as well to the Newberry Library special collections staff and to Newberry curator Will Hansen for research support and suggestions. Archival research for this article was supported by an Andrew W. Mellon / Lloyd Lewis fellowship at the Newberry Library.

1. Socrates, "Strictures," *Cherokee Phoenix,* March 13, 1828, 2.

2. Socrates, "Letter to the Editor," *Cherokee Phoenix,* July 10, 1830, 3.

3. Most recently, Ann McGrath has suggested that Socrates might be David or Joseph Vann, John Ridge, or another Cherokee person who had received a Western education. See McGrath, *Illicit Love: Interracial Sex and Marriage in the U.S. and Australia* (Lincoln: University of Nebraska Press, 2015), 164. In 2006, Claudio Saunt attributed the manuscript "Strictures" to Ridge but did not link the manuscript to its published version, attributed to Socrates. See Saunt, "Telling Stories: The Political Uses of Myth and History in the Cherokee and Creek Nations," *Journal of American History* 93, no. 3 (2006): 681–83.

4. The handwriting of the manuscript matches that of Ridge's other manuscript writings, which are held both in the Payne papers at the Newberry Library and in the Albert Gallatin papers at the New-York Historical Society.

5. See Daniel Heath Justice, *Our Fire Survives the Storm: A Cherokee Literary History* (Minneapolis: University of Minnesota Press, 2006), chap. 2; Tiya Miles, *The House on Diamond Hill: A Cherokee Plantation Story* (Chapel Hill: University of North Carolina Press, 2010); Theda Perdue, *Slavery and the Evolution of Cherokee Society, 1540–1866* (Knoxville: University of Tennessee Press, 1979); and Perdue, *Cherokee Women: Gender and Culture Change, 1700–1835* (Lincoln: University of Nebraska Press, 1998). For an older study, see William G. McLoughlin, *Cherokee Renascence in the New Republic* (Princeton, N.J.: Princeton University Press, 1986).

6. On Ridge's education (and that of Cherokee students, more broadly), see Hilary E. Wyss, *English Letters and Indian Literacies: Reading, Writing, and New England Missionary Schools, 1750–1830* (Philadelphia: University of

Pennsylvania Press, 2012), esp. chap. 4; on Ridge's and especially Boudinot's speeches, see Maureen Konkle, *Writing Indian Nations: Native Intellectuals and the Politics of Historiography, 1827–1863* (Chapel Hill: University of North Carolina Press, 2004), chap. 1.

7. For two recent discussions of the Treaty Party, see Justice, *Our Fire Survives the Storm,* esp. chaps. 2–3; and Joshua B. Nelson, *Identity in Cherokee Literature and Culture* (Norman: University of Oklahoma Press, 2014), chaps. 4–5.

8. Socrates, "Intermarriages," *Cherokee Phoenix,* March 27, 1828, 2; and Socrates, "Letter to the Editor," 3.

9. "A Cherokee" has letters in the *Phoenix* on February 28, 1828; March 20, 1828; July 21, 1828; May 6, 1828; June 4, 1828; and February 11, 1829; "A Cherokee Farmer" writes on March 11 and 18, 1829.

10. William Sturtevant, "John Ridge on Cherokee Civilization in 1826," *Journal of Cherokee Studies* 6 (1981): 79–91. For readings of Ridge's letter in the context of the Treaty of New Echota, see Konkle, *Writing Indian Nations,* 47. See also Theda Perdue and Michael D. Green, eds., *The Cherokee Removal: A Brief History with Documents* (New York: Bedford / St. Martin's, 1995), intro. and 31–33.

11. *Cherokee Nation v. State of Georgia,* 30 U.S. 1 (1831), *Justia US Supreme Court,* http://supreme.justia.com, n.d.

12. Robert Allen Warrior, *Tribal Secrets: Recovering American Indian Intellectual Traditions* (Minneapolis: University of Minnesota Press, 1995), esp. 91.

13. Ibid., 124; and Scott Richard Lyons, "Rhetorical Sovereignty: What Do American Indians Want from Writing?" *College Composition and Communication* 51, no. 3 (2000): 447–68.

14. The speech was reportedly first printed in the *Charleston Intelligencer* and reprinted in the *Boston Recorder,* vol. 7, December 28, 1822, 205. The transcript was made by an anonymous reporter, not Ridge himself. The speech highlights Ridge's education through references to British natural philosophers and Greek philosophers, but it also makes claims about Native nations' certain vanishing if they are not "attached" to missionaries, and it argues that Native nations should become part of the United States. In all his other writings, Ridge consistently argues precisely the opposite points. It is possible that missionaries from the American Board of Commissioners for Foreign Missions wrote the speech or required Ridge to copy points from other speeches or writings, a practice that would certainly align with the educational practice at Cornwall, which taught students through repetition and imitation. Indeed, parts of the speech match exactly an essay on the "Comparative Happiness of Civilized and Savage Life." While the only printing of this essay I have been able to locate is in Henry Mandeville's *Fourth Reader: For Common Schools and Academics* (New York, 1850), it is likely that this essay circulated in the 1820s in textbooks available to Ridge and his missionary teachers (nineteenth-century textbooks frequently reprinted poems and essays; see, for example, *The American Reader* [Poughkeepsie, 1812], one of the books used at Cornwall Mission School).

15. *Boston Recorder,* vol. 7, December 28, 1822, 205.

16. Isaac Watts, *The Improvement of the Mind. To which is added, A discourse on the education of children and youth. By Isaac Watts. D.D. From the last London*

edition (New York, 1819), 109. Watts was also the author of a widely used and influential hymnbook, *Hymns and Spiritual Songs* (first published in London, 1707). On the Socratic method in America, see also Jack Schneider, "Remembrance of Things Past: A History of the Socratic Method in the United States," *Curriculum Inquiry* 43, no. 5 (2013): 613–40.

17. Watts, *Improvement of the Mind*, 109.

18. Ibid., 108.

19. James Burnet, Lord Monboddo, *Of the Origin and Progress of Language*, vol. 5 (Edinburgh, 1773), 298.

20. Ibid., 298–99.

21. A search for "Socrates" in the database *America's Historical Newspapers* resulted in about 2,100 results. I limited this search to the years 1800–1830 and to newspapers in Georgia, South Carolina, Massachusetts, and Connecticut (states in which Ridge and Boudinot attended school or through which they traveled to speak; or states whose newspapers would have been likely circulate in the Cherokee Nation, thanks to Cherokee sources, ministers, or other white travelers). On Boudinot as editor, see Theda Perdue, ed., *Cherokee Editor: The Writings of Elias Boudinot* (Knoxville: University of Tennessee Press, 1983).

22. *Washington Reporter* (Washington, Pa.), January 14, 1822, 1.

23. Craig S. Womack, *Red on Red: Native American Literary Separatism* (Minneapolis: University of Minnesota Press, 1999), chap. 5. See also Alexander Posey, *The Fus Fixico Letters*, eds. Daniel F. Littlefield, Jr., and Carol A. Petty Hunter (Lincoln: University of Nebraska Press), 1993.

24. David S. Shields, *Civil Tongues and Polite Letters in British America* (Chapel Hill: University of North Carolina Press, 1997), 264.

25. Ridge gave over a dozen speeches between 1822 and 1832, and they were frequently summarized in newspapers along the East Coast, including in the Southeast and in the *Cherokee Phoenix*. Many papers reprinted accounts of these speeches from newspapers in cities where Ridge had given speeches, with the result that Ridge would have been known even in cities in which he had not spoken. He did publish several articles in the *Phoenix* under his own name, most notably in 1828 a response to Thomas L. McKenney, superintendent of Indian Affairs, who had accused Ridge of influencing Creek decisions regarding a renegotiated treaty for his own benefit. See *Cherokee Phoenix*, June 25, 1828, 2–3, and July 2, 1828, 2. Finally, a note in the March 18, 1829, *Phoenix* attests to the "unquestionable veracity" of "A Cherokee Farmer," suggesting that Boudinot and others involved in publishing the paper knew the identities of the pseudonymous writers (2).

26. Phillip H. Round, *Removable Type: Histories of the Book in Indian Country, 1663–1880* (Chapel Hill: University of North Carolina Press, 2010), 137–38.

27. Shields, *Civil Tongues and Polite Letters*, 264.

28. Socrates, "Strictures," March 13, 1828, 2.

29. "Indian Literature," *Vermont Watchman and State Gazette*, April 12, 1831, 1.

30. Socrates, "Strictures," *Cherokee Phoenix*, February 28, 1828, 2.

31. For a view of anonymity as desirable, see Michael Warner, *The Letters of*

the Republic: Publication and the Public Sphere in Eighteenth-Century America (Cambridge, Mass.: Harvard University Press, 1990), chap. 2. Warner's argument about anonymity has been critiqued by Trish Loughran, *The Republic in Print: Print Culture in the Age of U.S. Nation Building, 1770–1870* (New York: Columbia University Press, 2009).

32. Womack, *Red on Red,* 139–40.

33. Ibid., 153.

34. *Johnson & Graham's Lessee v. M'Intosh, U.S. Supreme Court,* 21 U.S. (8 Wheat.) 543, 1823, *Justia US Supreme Court,* http://supreme.justia.com, n.d.

35. David E. Wilkins and K. Tsianina Lomawaima, *Uneven Ground: American Indian Sovereignty and Federal Law* (Norman: University of Oklahoma Press, 2001), 54.

36. Ibid.

37. Ibid., 58

38. Henry Knox, "Report on the Northwestern Indians, June 15, 1789," in *Documents of U.S. Indian Policy,* ed. Francis Paul Prucha, 3rd ed. (Lincoln: University of Nebraska Press, 2000), 12–13.

39. "Treaty of Holston, 1791," *Cherokee Nation,* http://www.cherokee.org, n.d.

40. See Thomas Jefferson to William Henry Harrison, February 27, 1803, in *Documents of U.S. Indian Policy,* ed. Prucha, 22–23.

41. Knox, "Report," 13.

42. Jefferson to Harrison, 22–23.

43. Knox, "Report," 13.

44. Konkle, *Writing Indian Nations,* 17.

45. See Miles, *House on Diamond Hill,* 53. As Justice points out, some Cherokees chose to adopt some Western practices as a response to keep a "ravenous empire" at bay. See Justice, *Our Fire Survives the Storm,* 40.

46. *Report of a Committee, and Resolutions of the Legislature of the State of Georgia, in Relation to Certain Lands Occupied by the Cherokee Indians, Belonging to the Said State* (Washington, D.C., 1828).

47. Socrates, "Strictures," March 13, 1828, 2.

48. Emmerich de Vattel, *The Law of Nations, or Principles of the Law of Nature Applied to the Conduct and Affairs of Nations and Sovereigns* (London, 1797), 99.

49. Socrates, "Strictures," March 13, 1828, 2.

50. Mark Rifkin, *Manifesting America: The Imperial Construction of U.S. National Space* (New York: Oxford University Press, 2009), 17.

51. For this perspective, see Saunt, "Telling Stories."

52. Compiling notes or quotations from published texts, usually into manuscript or printed reference books but also into new texts, was a well-established practice by the nineteenth century, one Ridge would have encountered at Cornwall Mission School, where he created a commonplace book. As Ann Blair has pointed out, compilers were not "simple copyists but transformed the material as they disseminated it," by grouping quotations from different texts together, adding subheadings, or recontextualizing excerpts to invite interpretations different from those of a quotation in its original context. See Ann Blair, *Too Much*

to Know: Managing Scholarly Information before the Modern Age (New Haven, Conn.: Yale University Press, 2011), 176.

53. Vattel, *Law of Nations,* 100.

54. Ibid.

55. *Johnson & Graham's Lessee v. M'Intosh, U.S. Supreme Court.*

56. Socrates, "Strictures," March 13, 1828, 2. Socrates's discussion of Vattel and Hewatt may have influenced Jeremiah Evarts, the American Board of Foreign Missions secretary who in 1829 wrote a series of letters for the *National Intelligencer* in which he argued against Cherokee removal under the pseudonym William Penn. In letter 15, Penn reinterprets Vattel, and in letter 17, he uses Oglethorpe to discuss U.S. treaty responsibilities. Socrates's earlier discussion of these writers suggests that he may have served as a source or inspiration for Evarts, who, given his role overseeing Cornwall Mission School when Ridge was in attendance and his support for the Cherokees in the 1820s, would certainly have read the *Phoenix* and may have been one of the readers who knew Socrates's identity. See Francis Paul Prucha, ed., *Cherokee Removal: The "William Penn" Essays and Other Writings* (Knoxville: University of Tennessee Press, 1981).

57. Socrates, "Strictures," March 13, 1828, 2.

58. Ibid., February 28, 1828, 2.

59. "empire, n. and adj., 5a.," *OED Online,* http://www.oed.com, June 2016.

60. "empire," 3. Ibid.

61. Socrates, "Strictures," March 13, 1828, 2. All subsequent quotations in this paragraph are from the same source.

62. Ibid. All subsequent quotations in this paragraph are from the same source.

63. For a consideration of non-linear forms in a history of science context, see James Delbourgo and Staffan Müller-Wille, "Introduction," *Isis* 103, no. 4 (2012): 710–15.

64. Socrates, "Letter to the Editor," 3.

65. "Trade and Intercourse Act, March 30, 1802," *Documents of U.S. Indian Policy*, ed. Prucha, 19.

66. Socrates, "Letter to the Editor," 3.

67. Socrates, "Strictures," March 13, 1828, 2.

68. Ibid.

69. Ibid., July 10, 1830, 3.

70. Ibid., February 28, 1828, 2.

71. Ibid.

72. Ian Hunter, "Vattel in Revolutionary America: From the Rules of War to the Rule of Law," in *Between Indigenous and Settler Governance,* eds. Lisa Ford and Tim Rowse (New York: Routledge, 2013), 14.

73. Ibid.

74. See McGrath, *Illicit Love*; Theda Perdue: "Clan and Court: Another Look at the Early Cherokee Republic," *American Indian Quarterly* 24, no. 4 (2000): 562–69; and Fay Yarborough, "Legislating Women's Sexuality: Cherokee Marriage Laws in the Nineteenth Century," *Journal of Social History* 38, no. 2 (2004): 385–406.

75. Yarborough, "Legislating Women's Sexuality," 387—89.

76. See McGrath, *Illicit Love,* 157—58.

77. Socrates, "Intermarriages."

78. Audra Simpson, *Mohawk Interruptus: Political Life across the Borders of Settler States* (Durham, N.C.: Duke University Press, 2014), 12.

79. Ibid.

80. Socrates, "Strictures," February 28, 1828, 2.

81. Ibid., March 13, 1828, 2.

82. John Ridge to Elliot Cressen, February 6, 1831, *Vermont Watchman and State Gazette,* April 12, 1831, 1.

83. For articles rejecting accounts of Cherokees supporting removal, see the *Boston Recorder,* December 22 1830 (this article was republished in the *Cherokee Phoenix,* January 15, 1831, 3). For accusations that Ridge supported removal for his own benefit, see the *Albany Argus,* June 15, 1832, 2 (the *Argus* reprinted this article from a New Jersey paper, suggesting that these rumors circulated through practices of reprinting).

84. See the *Cherokee Phoenix,* November 23, 1833, 1—2.

85. Ibid., 2. All subsequent quotations in this paragraph are from the same source.

86. See Daniel F. Littlefield, Jr., and James W. Parins, *Native American Writing in the Southeast: An Anthology, 1875—1935* (Jackson: University Press of Mississippi, 1995), 30—47.

87. D. W. C. Duncan, "Story of the Cherokees," *Cherokee Advocate,* October 6, 1882, 1.

88. Ibid., October 27, 1882, 1.

89. Warrior, *Tribal Secrets,* 88.

KARRMEN CREY

Screen Text and Institutional Context: Indigenous Film Production and Academic Research Institutions

Introduction

NAVAJO TALKING PICTURE (Arlene Bowman 1986) and *Cry Rock* (Banchi Hanuse 2010) are documentaries exhibiting striking thematic similarities: both are made by Indigenous women emerging from university contexts who seek closer contact with their Indigenous cultural heritage. The filmmakers' relationships with their grandmothers manifest a cultural disconnect: while their grandmothers are fluent in their traditional languages, neither filmmaker is a speaker. The gap in language proficiency gestures to a cultural and social rupture that has taken place in the interceding generation. The generational ruptures experienced by Indigenous peoples under colonialism are well-known: efforts to eradicate traditional social organization through reservation/reserve systems and residential/boarding schools—among other legal, institutional, and physical methods—were designed to destroy Indigenous peoples' cultures and assimilate them into colonial settler society. As a part of this process, boarding school and residential school systems were created and separated Indigenous children from their families and communities, forcing children to adopt colonial settler values and cultural practices. These schools sought to eradicate Indigenous languages in particular, often using corporeal punishment to prevent students from speaking their traditional languages.[1] As a result, a generation suffered massive cultural and social disruption that is represented by generational differences in Indigenous language speakers. This crux is the central motif for both films, through which they investigate the applications of the cinematic apparatus for connecting Indigenous people to their communities and cultural heritage.

Their methods for engaging and representing these topics are, however, very different, drawing from frameworks for undertaking Indigenous research that emerged from distinct historical periods and national contexts. Bowman produced *Navajo Talking Picture* in the early 1980s through the University of California, Los Angeles film production program in association with the American Indian Studies Center (AISC); *Cry Rock* was deeply informed by Hanuse's experience in the First Nations Studies Program (FNSP)[2] at the University of British Columbia in the mid-2000s, and her experience in media-based project development at the National Film Board of Canada (NFB). For *Navajo Talking Picture,* the reinvention of film-based anthropology that began in the 1960s intersected with developments in Indigenous studies during the same era to engender a research environment in which it was understood that Indigenous people are best equipped to undertake research on Indigenous people and topics, a frame of reference that the film examines and complicates via Bowman's interactions with her grandmother, Ann Biah. Made twenty years later, *Cry Rock* engages with debates in Indigenous studies about the relationship between oral narrative traditions and the media used to record them, questioning the impact that recording technologies have on oral narratives and their survival. By doing so, the film intervenes in assumptions that the cinematic apparatus can function as an extension of oral traditions, a discourse promoted by the NFB, raising the possibility that recording technologies actually hasten their erosion. *Cry Rock* ultimately explores oral narratives as a mode of understanding that is intrinsically tied to specific geographical places and relies on a direct relationship between storyteller and listener, which media technologies cannot replicate.

Bringing together *Navajo Talking Picture* and *Cry Rock* is in part a means by which to argue that analyses of the thematic similarities between media texts should be attentive to institutional contexts that Indigenous media practitioners navigate in their work, an approach that draws on precedent studies of minority media by Chon Noriega (2000) and Jun Okada (2015). Their work on Chicano cinema and Asian American film and video, respectively, has sought to understand minority cinemas not as pre-given, identity-based categories, but as areas of production debated and shaped through various social forces, including state policy, political movements, developments in media technologies, and institutional funding structures and policies. At stake are the terms through which minority media are conceptualized, as Noriega argues, as identity-based cinematic "genres": "What must be repressed in such a move is the fact that one is doing a form of genre analysis that effectively reduces institutional analysis and social history to a textual effect; that is, these social phenomena exist only as signs circulating within a closed set of texts" (21). Noriega here delineates the inherent limitations of approaching minority media as "genres," which transforms social phenomena into textual features that come to constitute sets of characteristics through which these media texts are recognized. This approach can circumscribe interpretation of this work to registering sociocultural markers of difference associated with minority groups and politics at the expense of other axes of analysis that contextualize these media texts, including institutional discourses and production practices. I focus on the institutional relationships for *Navajo Talking Picture* and *Cry Rock* to argue that institutions of media culture are a part of Indigenous media practitioners' sociocultural contexts, and influence the textual features and representational strategies of Indigenous screen content.

This approach also owes to research on the social context of Indigenous media that has been taken up in anthropology, where work by Eric Michaels (1994), Faye Ginsburg (1991, 1994), Kristen Dowell (2013), and Sigurjon Baldur Hafsteinsson (2008), among others, has shifted attention away from screen content, arguing that confining understandings of Indigenous media to its textual features overlooks the social relations that production enables and supports. Here, Indigenous media is understood as a form of cultural mediation that, as Ginsburg (1991, 94) states, "offers a possible means—social, cultural and political—for reproducing and transforming cultural identity among people who have experienced massive, political, geographic and economic disruption." I argue that *institutions* are a part of Indigenous media's social dynamics, and have historically played a critical role in providing funding and programs for Indigenous production. Such institutions include national film agencies, art galleries, professional training programs, and broadcasters. While these institutions do not necessarily dictate the terms of Indigenous production, they do produce discourses of Indigeneity that shape their funding structures, institutional policies, and representational practices, which Indigenous filmmakers negotiate in the production of their work. Drawing on records and public materials from academic and cultural institutions, I explore the material and discursive contexts that Bowman and Hanuse negotiate in their films, and how these negotiations are inscribed in the films themselves. As a result, this approach seeks to bring together analysis of Indigenous media's social relations with the text itself.

Practice-Based Film Education and Indigenous Studies

By attending to debates in Indigenous studies and their effects on film produced in relation to academic research institutions, this article engages somewhat elliptically but productively with scholarship from film school studies or practice-based film education, which seeks to understand "how filmmakers become filmmakers" (Hjort 2013, 1). Scholarship in this area has historically tended to consider a filmmaker's education in terms of two institutional models: the "conservatoire" that is typically founded as a part of a national film industry, and the university department, which is a part of a "larger educational establishment and therefore constrained and guided by the academic policies and practices of that institution" (Petrie 2010, 34). Petrie explains that both models seek a theoretically informed production practice that has "sought to combine hands-on filmmaking and an intellectual framework that embraces the theory, criticism, and history of cinema, providing students with a context for locating and understanding their own creative practice." To this I would add that such intellectual frameworks must also consider the theory, criticism, and history of disciplinary areas *outside* of film areas, but which nonetheless inform production. Students, faculty, and administrators bring their experiences from different social and educational arenas into film practice, contributing to the development and evolution of film education, circumstances that Mette Hjort outlines in her introduction to *The Education of the Filmmaker in Africa, the Middle East, and the Americas* (2013, 4), where she states that "there can be no one-to-one correspondence between the profile of a given film school on the one hand, and the priorities and values of its graduates on the other. After all, film schools are subject to the full range of complexities that characterize institutional life. . . . If being a filmmaker is the outcome of a process of becoming, factors shaping that process are not merely to be sought in the institutional landscape of film schools and practice-based training programs" (4). The complicated "ecology" (11) of practice-based film education that Hjort describes is important for contextualizing Bowman's and Hanuse's films, which engage with intellectual frameworks from other areas of postsecondary institutions and other institutions of media production. Their institutional "unwieldiness" is generative, however, as it makes visible the ways in which intellectual frameworks and practices from academic research institutions intersect with and put pressure on the discourses and practices in other areas and institutions.

Navajo Talking Picture *(1986)*

Navajo Talking Picture is perhaps best known in Indigenous cinema history for its controversial depiction of its filmmaker's interactions with her grandmother, Ann Biah. The documentary was Bowman's thesis film for her MFA degree in film production at UCLA. Bowman, a Diné (Navajo) woman, was raised away from her family's Diné community, and set out to create an ethnographic film of the daily life of her grandmother, who speaks only the Diné language and largely eschews a Western lifestyle and conveniences.[3] In the film's voice-over, Bowman explains that she intended to create a portrait of her grandmother and her lifestyle, but that after several days of filming, her grandmother stopped cooperating with the film crew and asked them to leave. Bowman, unable to speak the Diné language, did not understand her grandmother's objections and returned to the reservation several times to continue filming. The film is reflexive about her efforts and frustrations: she narrates her confusion with her grandmother's behavior, and attributes her hostility to being misperceived as a "big shot" from Los Angeles who is bent on exploitation.

For Bowman, the film's central conflict emerged from cultural differences between herself and her traditional grandmother. The film portrays Bowman as very much urban and cosmopolitan: she lives in Los Angeles, wears youthful and stylish clothing, and attends UCLA. Her grandmother, meanwhile, is shown living in a small hogan without plumbing or electricity, weaving wool rugs, and periodically traveling to the local store for provisions. Their cultural divide is compounded by their inability to speak the same language, which, Bowman explains in the film, exacerbated tensions between them. Ultimately, Bowman incites a confrontation with her grandmother in the climactic moment of the film where she ambushes her in her home, accompanied by the film crew and translator. Through the translator, Bowman tries to explain her intentions to her grandmother and find out why she is so resistant, while Biah tries to evade them, telling them to leave. The scene is extremely charged and, as Randolph Lewis has detailed, the focus for much debate and criticism.

In *Navajo Talking Picture: Cinema on Native Ground* (2012, 79), Lewis identifies that critiques of the film largely focus on the filmmaker's "ethical lapses" owing to her persistence in filming despite her grandmother's clearly stated refusal to participate. Such critiques, he argues, overlook how Bowman's

FIGURE 1. Arlene Bowman at UCLA in *Navajo Talking Picture*.

FIGURE 2. Ann Biah in her kitchen in *Navajo Talking Picture*.

techniques are typical of prevailing filmmaking practices, and cover over its interventions in critical paradigms attending Indigenous identity and cultural production. Lewis discusses, for instance, the film's relationship to family portrait films in which intergenerational conflict is a central feature, often thematized by tensions between the filmmaker and their family members' reluctance to engage with the camera (114–15). By showing that such techniques are characteristic of the genre, Lewis seeks to reveal the film's complex textuality, "bracketing" criticism in order to make visible the film's contributions to understandings of Indigenous identity, art, and ethics. He argues that *Navajo Talking Picture* intervenes in major critical paradigms in Indigenous studies that he critiques for making essentialist claims about Indigenous identity and art: "tribalcentric criticism" and "Indigenous aesthetics." Both paradigms, Lewis argues, are premised on "authenticity" as a means to recognize and legitimize Indigenous artists and their work. In his view, tribalcentric criticism, which emerged from Indigenous literary nationalism, is "a sort of aesthetic nationalism in which tribal citizens, or at least those fluent with the culture's history and language, are ideally positioned to appreciate a work of art that originates among its ranks" (133) and risks "granting critical authority solely by virtue of biography" (136). Indigenous aesthetics, he states, is a concept that has been enigmatically described as an underlying "logic" to Indigenous cultural production, or as a set of characteristics appearing in this work, including intergenerational continuity, respect for elders, a sense of community, a schema that does not accommodate work by Indigenous artists lacking such features (140). Looking at Bowman and *Navajo Talking Picture* through these critical lenses makes visible their limitations, as they cannot accommodate her "liminality" as an Indigenous person, nor account for the film's problematic representation of Bowman's grandmother. Doing so, Lewis argues, allows him to produce an "anti-essentialist" reading of the film that defines its major contribution to understandings of Indigenous identity and art: "Indigenous filmmakers face the same hazards as any other documentarians working in the field, and that to assign them special representational powers (or a unique aesthetic) is as misguided as the limiting notions that portray them as spiritual, wise, or close to nature. Unless they choose otherwise, Native filmmakers have no special purchase on accountability to their subjects but instead operate like artists anywhere, able to persist long into the night with ill-advised plans for wrong-headed projects just like anyone else" (142). Lewis's intent is to make visible Bowman's complicated identity as a Diné person, and thereby recover her from criticism emerging from essentialist assumptions about what an Indigenous filmmaker is "supposed to be." Doing so makes it possible to appreciate the human dimensions of her flawed endeavor, and the way the film raises important questions about the applications and limitations of critical paradigms in Indigenous studies. At the same time, it is not clear that all criticism of the film's ethical issues comes from the same essentialist assumptions about Indigenous identity. Lewis brings together non-Indigenous students' responses to in-class screenings with those of Indigenous scholar Beverly Singer (2001), though there are differences between the perceptions of students who have a limited grasp of Indigenous issues, and those of an Indigenous academic firmly grounded in the field. Singer's analysis is attentive to Ann Biah's perspective in order to identify the cultural and historical underpinnings to her responses, arguing that Biah's inability to fend off the camera "is reminiscent also of history when Native people were unable to defend themselves against white encroachment. Bowman's grandmother appears to be in her seventies; in her youth she would have heard stories about the campaign against the Navajo and of the 'Navajo Long Walk'" (77).[4] By linking Biah's responses to the Diné history of forced relocation, Singer exposes layers of unvoiced traumas that Bowman's interactions with her grandmother invoke. I understand her critique as a pedagogical one, and as a part of the drive of Indigenous academics and researchers to bring scholarly attention to Indigenous histories and issues. Lewis raises valuable questions about studies of audience demographics and reception for Indigenous media that deserve more attention; however, this is not his project here. Rather, he is interested in unpacking the way the film complicates essentialist discourses that attend studies of Indigenous media, and reception of the film as one possible source of such discourses.

Lewis centers an Indigenous film "outlier" to demonstrate the pressure that the film and Bowman herself place on critical frameworks in Indigenous studies, providing a compelling analytical model that I build on by bringing institutional analysis into the interpretive fold. As a film emerging from an academic research institution, it speaks to beliefs and practices for undertaking Indigenous research contemporaneous with its production circulating in Indigenous studies, anthropology, and ethnographic film at UCLA. Lewis touches on ethnography in his analysis of *Navajo Talking Picture*, acknowledging the work's original intent to be an "ethnographic film," but more so as a means of attenuating criticism of the film's ethics by arguing that such critiques are anachronistic when considering the film in light of documentary trends of the era (i.e., family portrait films). Thus, Lewis's analysis shifts away from ethnography and attendant questions of ethics in order to contextualize the film and examine its textual plurality. Institutional analysis, however, re-centers questions of ethics by examining the film's contributions to understandings about research and knowledge production of Indigenous peoples. Examining the intersections of ethnography and documentary film at UCLA, complemented by Bowman's training in still photography, contributes to understandings of the film's representational strategies for depicting cross-cultural conflict between Indigenous people.

The Reinvention of Anthropology and Colonial Legacies of Indigenous Images

Bowman describes the rationale for the film in annual progress reports submitted to the UCLA American Indian Studies Center, a research unit that provided funding to assist her project from 1982 to 1986, and in interviews conducted in 2015 reflecting on these reports and her experience making the film. The reports detail Bowman's progress, difficulties encountered in the filming process, and her reasons for employing particular approaches to address them. Though these challenges are documented within the film itself, the reports are revealing of the ethnographic and documentary discourses through which the project was designed and to which it was responsive. In interviews, Bowman also describes the influence of still photography on the film, demonstrating the confluence of photography-based and ethnographic practice.

The first annual report from 1983 indicates that the project was intended to be a portrait of her grandmother, Ann Biah, but explains that her grandmother's lack of cooperation and interaction motivated her decision to include herself in the film because "in an ethnographic, direct cinematic film, if the film depiction of a person's daily life does not interact with other people a lot, the film looks less interesting" (Bowman 1983, 68). Moreover, the choice to include herself in the film was a reflexive move intended to "make the connection between both our worlds," indicating that the film shifted from an "ethnographic, direct cinematic film" (ibid.) to, as Bowman describes in an interview, a "personal documentary" (2015a). For Bowman, the "personal documentary" dispenses with objectivity and is instead defined by her point of view, which was enacted by reflexively inserting herself into the film in order to focus on issues affecting the progress of the film, which were thematized as issues of cross-cultural dynamics. Bowman links this approach with the genre of self-portraiture in relation to her training in still photography: "I remember being introduced to it a little bit by a teacher in high school, about still photography's history . . . I know still photographers take self-portraits . . . That's probably why it influenced me" (ibid.). While Bowman describes a personal dimension to her entry into the film as a form of "self-portraiture," this approach intersects with a long colonial history of the Diné people in photography and film that contributed to tensions during production. Throughout the film, Bowman is aligned with Western colonial practices, particularly the history of exploitation in Western visual culture. In her 1983 report, Bowman states that family and community members told her grandmother that she should not be filmed and that Bowman was "exploiting her," suggesting that Bowman was aware that Diné community members interpreted her project along a continuum of colonial practices. Lewis includes a comprehensive summary of the history of colonial fascination with images of "the Navajo" in portraiture, Hollywood cinema, and anthropology, which has generated a substantial body of scholarship examining Diné relationships to visual culture, as both "objects" of its gaze and as agents in its production and reception.[5] James C. Faris (1996) examines the extent to which the Diné have been the object of photography, first as a part of nineteenth- and twentieth-century ethnographic investigations of the colonial "Other," and increasingly in the twentieth century as tourist curiosities when photographic technologies became available to a mobile American population—so much so that "the impression is that few people crossed northwestern New Mexico and northern Arizona without pointing a camera at Navajo" (150). While recognizing Faris's important analysis of the visual regimes through which Indigenous people have been subject to the colonial gaze, subsequent scholarship has been more closely attentive to Diné agency throughout this history and in their relationships to film and photography.[6] Lewis (2012) and Limbrick (2010) examine Hollywood productions filmed in Diné territory that employed Diné actors and extras, and the negotiations between the Navajo Nation and these productions in which they defined the terms of their participation. This literature overwhelmingly indicates that the Diné people possess a sophisticated understanding of the ideological and economic interests of photography and filmmaking, and that this knowledge motivates their wariness of Bowman's project. Thus, while *Navajo Talking Picture* uses "self-portraiture" to intervene in colonial representational practices, this approach did not resolve them; instead, it brought to light complexities and striations internal to the Diné people resulting from colonial history.

Minority Media Histories and Indigenous Studies

As a photographer by training, Bowman brought a background in visual arts to bear on a film that was aligned with traditions of ethnographic filmmaking and direct cinema, which speaks to the history of minority-directed film production at the University of California, Los Angeles that largely took shape through the Ethno-Communications Program founded in the late 1960s. As David E. James details in *The Most Typical Avant-Garde: History and Geography of Minor Cinemas in Los Angeles* (2005), the Ethno-Communications Program emerged in the context of the civil rights movement in the 1960s, and particularly the Watts Rebellion in Los Angeles in 1965. In response to these social pressures, UCLA founded ethnic studies centers and programs, and began recruiting students from minority groups, specifically African American, Asian American, Chicano, and Native American students. The ethnic studies centers were designed to support minority groups' greater control of and representation in research.

For the American Indian Studies Center at UCLA (AISC), this has meant working toward self-determination for Indigenous people by "soliciting Indian priorities for research, training Indian researchers . . . and disseminating accurate information about American Indian peoples" (UCLA American Indian Studies Center 1980, 3). This statement voices founding principles of Indigenous studies as it took shape in North America. Elizabeth Cook-Lynn (1997, 10) dates the discipline to the late 1960s and early 1970s and the interdisciplinary efforts of Indigenous academics, professional personnel, artists, and traditional historians of the era to create an academic discipline in which "a body of intellectual information such as the Natives of this land possess about the world [would] be internally organized, normatively regulated, and consensually communicated." This body of knowledge is held in oral traditional narratives that are bound to the geographies of Indigenous nations from which they emerge. Therefore, Cook-Lynn argues, Indigenous studies is inherently invested in communal efforts to defend Indigenous nationhood (11). Cautioning that Indigenous studies cannot be conflated with other areas of ethnic studies, she identifies that Indigenous studies "would differentiate itself from other disciplines in two important ways: it would emerge from within Native people's enclaves and geographies, languages and experiences, and it would refute the exogenous seeking of truth through isolation (i.e., the 'ivory tower') that has been the general principle of the disciplines most recently in charge of indigenous study, that is, history, anthropology, and related disciplines all captivated by the scientific method of objectivity."

Thus, in its origins, the discipline gave rise to at least two premises: it positions Indigenous peoples as the source of expert knowledge, and therefore best equipped to produce research concerning Indigenous peoples, and undertakes research that works with and benefits Indigenous communities.[7] Bowman's project, funded by AISC, fits this mission. The film is framed as a research project in the AISC reports, with Bowman as principal investigator, and addresses AISC's goals of preparing Indigenous researchers to produce knowledge about Indigenous peoples. However, *Navajo Talking Picture* complicates these premises as they are applied in the historical world via documentary film.

Along with the founding of the ethnic studies centers, thirteen students and faculty at UCLA formed the Media Urban Crisis Committee in 1968 (also known as the "Mother Muccers") to advocate for access to film training and resources, resulting in a pilot film program that enrolled the Mother Muccers as its first students. The program was modeled on UCLA's already-established film production program, though it operated independently and had its own instructors and curriculum. The Ethno-Communications Program provided training and resources for minority students to represent their own interests and concerns and develop their own cinemas, a response to the exclusion of minorities from mainstream film industries, and to Hollywood cinema's frequently racist representations of minorities on screen (Hawkins 1970). The Ethno-Communications Program paved the way for filmmakers like Bowman, whose own film can be seen as emerging from this history and ethic.

Navajo Talking Picture's original ethnographic design likely emerged from the influence of ethnography and anthropology in film production at UCLA during this period, which overlapped in certain regards with the political and ideological commitments of Ethno-Communications. Colin Young, a visual anthropologist and ethnographic filmmaker at UCLA, was the first chair of the Media Urban Crisis Committee, and his colleague and fellow anthropologist, Richard Hawkins, was head of the Motion Picture Division of the Theater Arts Department (now the School for Theater, Film, and Television) as well as Bowman's supervisor for her film (Bowman 1983, 67). Young and Hawkins participated in the "reinvention" of anthropology in the 1960s and 1970s, motivated by the political and intellectual movements of the era that raised questions of the goals and methods of the discipline. Subsequent ethnographic work attempted more self-conscious processes that involved subjects in the production and interpretation of research.[8] Young and others recognized the influence of the ethnographer/filmmaker and camera on the behavior of their subjects, and argued that the film's subjects decided how to interact with the filmmaker in any scenario. The subjects therefore determined the film's project, and rather than projecting understandings of their subjects, the task of the ethnographer/filmmaker was to facilitate and make visible the negotiations between subject and filmmaker as a part of the filmmaking process. Bowman's original project design speaks to this ethnographic tradition, an attempt at more equitable, subject-directed interaction.

Forcing Interaction: The Crisis Structure

As Bowman relates in her report from 1983, however, her grandmother stopped interacting with her and the crew after several days of filming and ordered them to leave. Bowman's solution was to add "interaction" and "interest" by inserting herself into the film. She states that this would create the "drama and conflict needed for the film," and that through this forced interaction, "a sense of my grandmother's personality could be depicted" (1983, 68). She suggests that the conflict could produce a more dimensional representation of her grandmother, a technique owing to methods of direct cinema. In "Direct Cinema and the Crisis Structure," Stephen Mamber (1972) describes the function of the crisis structure in direct cinema of the 1960s as a way of revealing subjects' personalities, since a person's reaction to a crisis would reveal something of their character that would not be seen otherwise, resulting in a more multifaceted representation. Bowman echoes this logic when she states that "either she could have spoken to me or not spoken to me. She *reacts* in either case" (1983, 68; emphasis mine). The creation of a crisis structure was, in a sense, a functional solution to the scenario Bowman was facing to move the production forward.

A crisis structure also made it possible to thematize "cultural conflict" within the film, which Bowman identifies as the basis for her fraught interactions with her grandmother. Bowman explains in the 1983 report that "the appearance of myself in the film, literally opened interaction and made the connection between both of our worlds . . . she is coerced to speak to me. This is a central conflict and meeting of two cultures" (ibid.). In interviews, Bowman (2015c) describes experiencing a history of culture clashes, explaining it in terms of having been brought up in Phoenix, and then undertaking her training in photography in San Francisco, and contrasts these experiences with working on the Navajo reservation several years before undertaking her work at UCLA, which she describes as "isolating" owing to her struggles to live and work in a "small town" after living in urban spaces. She elaborates that this sense of a "culture clash" carried into the film, stating, "Maybe I didn't know enough about . . . Diné people who live on the reservation . . . I'm so frank, and so blatant, and I don't think many Diné people are blatant and frank" (ibid.). Bowman elaborated that her "frankness" took shape as a defense mechanism against the racism she experienced throughout her life, and the sexism she encountered while working in the film industry in southern California, where such forthrightness and assertiveness served her well; as she states, "I usually fight back with my words" (Bowman 2015b). Her demeanor was therefore a very rational response to the realities of living in settler-colonial society. In the context of her interactions with her grandmother and community, however, Bowman felt this same demeanor alienated her and exacerbated cultural tensions. By inserting herself in the film she not only "fixes" the problem of non-interaction, she also reflexively represents the cultural conflict that that she understood being the core of the film.

Bowman's reports also identify that her grandmother's resistance to being photographed was a part of cultural taboos against photography, adding another axis of "cultural conflict" structuring the film. In the 1983 report, she states that her grandmother "believed in traditional ways regarding camera and sound equipment," and that "a granddaughter is not supposed to film her grandmother" (68). She discovers this during her third visit to the reservation, which forms the penultimate scene of the film. Biah keeps her back to the camera and repeatedly tries to leave the room, while pursued by Bowman and the camera, with the translator awkwardly trailing along. Biah finally sits on her bed, turns away from the camera, and has the translator tell Bowman that the Diné never used to take photographs of their grandmothers, and also that when she was a child her grandfather told her stories that she remembered in her prayers; she never thought of taking pictures. Biah's response invokes cultural taboos against photography as explanation and context for her evasion of the camera, but also strategically addresses the immediate situation. When she explains that she remembers her grandfather's stories in her prayers, she identifies that she listened to him out of respect. She contrasts her actions to Bowman's: since Bowman is not listening to her grandmother, she is being disrespectful. While the film positions taboos against photography to emphasize the theme of "cultural conflict," the photographic apparatus is not the only issue here—more pressingly, it is Bowman's behavior.

Following the scene of the "crisis" encounter, Bowman is shown in a close-up outside the hogan, anxious and exhausted, debating with herself and someone behind the camera whether she "forced" her grandmother, followed by a scene of her in a pen of lambs, chasing one until she catches it and, laughing and breathless, shows it to the camera. This scene comments reflexively on her dogged pursuit of Biah, the reasons for which are alluded to in her reports. These reports track the film's development over at least four years, and show that the film represented a significant investment of time and financial and personal resources. The film itself identifies Bowman's financial hardship in a scene where she looks for work opportunities at the student financial aid office. As a thesis film, Bowman's M.F.A. degree depended on completing the project. The possibility of not finishing the film would mean a major personal and professional loss. These dimensions of her production provide a way of framing her persistence in the face of her grandmother's resistance and despite her own apprehensions.

The film concludes with an interior shot in Bowman's car as she and the crew drive away from the reservation, and in voice-over she reflects on the issues she felt were the basis for the conflict with her grandmother: the language barrier, her perception that her grandmother did not understand the project, and her own lack of understanding of Diné cultural and social prohibitions around photography. She states that she had set out to develop "understanding" between herself and her grandmother, and between herself and "the Navajo," a goal she felt had actually been realized to a degree in the film-making process. She states that she also came to understand the limitations of her own position: despite being a Diné woman, her lack of familiarity with Diné cultural values and history created problematic cultural dynamics that she attempted to address through reflexive techniques of inserting herself in the film and commenting on her upbringing in the "white world." This is one of the key insights of the film, pointing out that shared ethnicity and heritage does not translate into shared cultural values and understandings: there is not a unified Diné perspective. Such assumptions do not take into account the Indigenous peoples' historical realities of displacement and movement to urban areas to access resources not available on reservations, conditions underpinning the differences in Bowman's and Biah's cultural positions. Just as Lewis identifies that an Indigenous documentarian can make the same mistakes as any other documentarian, from an institutional standpoint it can be argued that the film makes the point that the power dynamics and representational issues of ethnographic practice are not necessarily resolved by involving a person of the same social or cultural position as their subjects; it is possible for researchers of Indigenous heritage to perform just as prob-lematically as non-Indigenous researchers, and therefore makes visible the need for attention to methodologies for producing knowledge about and rep-resenting Indigenous groups and issues. This insight makes it possible to pro-ductively foreground the film's ethical issues as a part of the film's insights.

Though these ethical lapses can be considered "productive," they are no less distressing to witness and worth reflecting on to examine the issues relevant to academic research they elicit. Lewis skillfully demonstrates how Bowman's techniques are not so different from those used in family portrait documentaries, and suggests that condemnation of the film is perhaps dis-proportionate when viewed within its historical context. As Lewis points out in his discussion of the reception of *Navajo Talking Picture,* viewers fre-quently condemn Bowman, responses that Bowman (1985, 46) alludes to from the first in her final report, which states that she found that audiences "did not fully understand what [she] was trying to present about the conflict and reasons between Arlene [Bowman] and the grandmother over the film-ing at the beginning of the film, when they should have." The language here is somewhat ambiguous, but it suggests that the issues of cultural conflict that emerged while Bowman attempted to create a portrait of her grandmother, and that Bowman sought to foreground, were overshadowed by the subse-quent direction of the film. These responses are shaped by expectations that the documentary genre bears a close relationship to historical and social re-ality, and therefore involve ethical considerations regarding their "subjects." Such ethical considerations are compounded when engaging with socially and historically marginalized people. It is reasonable to assume that most audiences understand that Indigenous peoples have been historically oppressed, particularly if they view the film in a classroom setting, where the instructor is likely to provide this context. Even a general appreciation of this history compounds the impact of film's "crisis," as it depicts the re-victimization of an Indigenous person by her own granddaughter. It is therefore instructive to consider how techniques used in prevailing documentary practices create different sets of issues when applied to the representation of Indigenous groups, not necessarily because of different expectations of the documentarian, but out of recognition of the social and historical specificities of Indigenous peoples' experiences and the legacies of colonization that these approaches can and do replicate. Therefore, methodologies for knowledge production, which documentaries and research share, require attention and debate prior to undertaking such projects, a process that *Cry Rock* (2010) examines as its structuring narrative.

Cry Rock *(2010)*

Navajo Talking Picture largely emerged in relation to one academic research institution, which has retained a set of production records that contribute to understandings of institutional discourses and representational practices that informed the film's development. *Cry Rock* engages dynamically with multiple institutional discourses and practices owing to its production history and context, which traces the filmmaker's professional experience in film and media production and in Indigenous studies at a postsecondary research institution. Thus, *Cry Rock* requires a broader framework for institutional analysis than *Navajo Talking Picture* in order to elicit how the film brings together representational practices and discourses of Indigeneity from multiple sites. Further, while records exist for *Navajo Talking Picture* that enrich institutional analysis, such records are not the sole sources through which institutional discourses can be read; in the case of *Cry Rock,* I draw on websites, reports, and publicity materials along with an interview with the filmmaker.

Cry Rock is a twenty-eight-minute documentary by Nuxalk filmmaker Banchi Hanuse, independently produced in 2010 by Smayaykila Films. Combining documentary footage with animation, the film begins at a point of urgency: there are only fifteen fluent Nuxalk language speakers and storytellers left, including Hanuse's grandmother. As Hanuse relates in voice-over, she cannot speak the language and wants to ask her grandmother if she can record her stories on camera; however, she cannot bring herself to ask. Instead, the film is an investigation of her apprehension, opening up an exploration of Nuxalk understandings of storytelling, and the potential repercussions of recording these stories using media and writing technologies. Her grandmother does appear in the film, though does not directly interact with the camera; instead, she is shown in a second narrative strand interwoven with the first in which she fillets and smokes a salmon.

Hanuse explains that she had been considering recording her grandmother for several years before undertaking the project, in the meantime undergoing film training largely at Capilanou University (Vancouver, B.C.) while gaining experience on film sets and at the NFB and complementing her professional training with First Nations Studies and International Relations at the University of British Columbia (UBC) (Hanuse 2015). While Hanuse's experience is diverse and multi-sited, for the purposes of this article I concentrate on the institutional locations closest temporally and contextually to the production of *Cry Rock*. Hanuse stated that her postsecondary education at UBC was "the base and the kick start . . . to continue to pursue film," and while at UBC she worked at the NFB as a producer, leading up to the production of *Cry Rock* (ibid.).

Hanuse recounted that "when contemplating recording elders, such as my grandmother, questions came to mind that concerned me. Thinking of my grandmother turning eighty, I realized there is so much knowledge my Grandmother has that I want to pass on" (ibid.). Historically, the Nuxalk language and stories were transmitted through oral traditional methods, and *Cry Rock* asks whether recordings can capture the meaning of the language and the stories—and whether, having been recorded, they can still be considered Indigenous cultural knowledge. The film ultimately presents cultural knowledge as a *modality,* and asks questions about what happens when certain forms of cultural knowledge are taken into a different cultural representational system. Indigenous languages emerge from cultural knowledge systems, and are understood as being key to transmitting traditional cultural knowledge. The Nuxalk language is endangered as a consequence of colonialism and the Canadian state's efforts to eradicate Indigenous cultures, which targeted Indigenous languages in particular. In *Cry Rock,* elders of Hanuse's grandmother's generation are shown to be fluent in Nuxalk, but we do not see people from Hanuse's *parents'* generation, a structuring absence that marks the break in language ability within that era. Questions about the effects of technology in cultural transmission thematize the generational cultural ruptures since, without the same language facility, these generations do not share the same framework for engaging traditional cultural knowledge. As a result, "mediation" is both a dominant visual motif and the focus for the film.

Inter-institutionality: Indigenous Studies and the National Film Board

Cry Rock's examination of the value and meaning of oral traditions, and the mediations that take place when oral narratives are recorded, reflect Indigenous studies debates taking place in the First Nations Studies Program at UBC, from which Hanuse graduated in 2004. FNSP is a research-oriented undergraduate program designed to equip students with theoretical and methodological skills in order to undertake Indigenous community-based research (First Nations Studies Program n.d.). Its core courses focus on research methodologies that debate methodological approaches for undertaking Indigenous research, which includes questions about the effects of recording technologies on Indigenous cultures. While Hanuse was a student in the program in 2003, a unit of the required course "FNSP 310: Theory Seminar" focused on technologies and their effects on Indigenous peoples, including readings from Jerry Mander's *In the Absence of the Sacred: The Failure of Technology and the Survival of the Indian Nations* (1992) and Elise Mather's "With a Vision Beyond Our Needs: Oral Traditions in an Age of Literacy" (1995); further, the course asked students to examine "the relation between technology and First Nations cultures" in a written or media-based assignment (Kesler 2003a). "FNSP 320: Research Methods," a second required course, engaged even more deeply with debates surrounding research methods, and includes workshops and readings on research ethics—including Linda Tuhiwai Smith's foundational text *Decolonizing Methodologies: Research and Indigenous Peoples* (1999)—in preparation for students' major assignment, an interview-based research project (Kesler 2003b). *Cry Rock* echoes these debates in its questioning of the applications and limitations of recording technologies for preserving and transmitting Indigenous cultural knowledge, a critical framework dovetailing with Hanuse's long-held deliberations about whether to record her grandmother's stories.

These debates intervene in and complicate institutional discourses around Indigenous cultural retention that circulate at the National Film Board of Canada, where Hanuse worked throughout the 2000s, and which was an associate producer of *Cry Rock*. Hanuse was the coproducer and project coordinator of *Our World,* an Indigenous language—based program that took shape in the early 2000s out of NFB's West Coast—based Pacific and Yukon Centre (Hanuse 2015). *Our World* partnered the NFB with remote Indigenous communities in British Columbia and the Yukon to teach youth how to use digital technologies in order to make short films in their traditional languages (National Film Board of Canada 2011).[9] Filmmakers and digital animators visited communities whose traditional languages are endangered, and worked with youth aged eighteen to twenty-nine to develop projects that would engage with their traditional languages in ways relevant to their experiences, as described by the project's archived website: "*Our World* is based on the concept of giving voice and inviting others to hear. The project aims to leave something behind that benefits both the individual and the community. By facilitating active communication and reception, we encourage positive social engagement. It is also about exposing young people to potential future career options by learning how to express themselves creatively with modern, digital media" (ibid.). Social engagement and empowerment predominate as discursive frameworks for the project, wherein media technology acts as a facilitator that supports Indigenous people's connections with their cultures and communities. The "social engagement" framework is enhanced by the language of professionalization, in which participants would be equipped with skills transferrable to the employment realm.

This social engagement framework echoes long-established NFB discourses for minority and Indigenous production. As Zoë Druick (2007) argued, the NFB, as a national film agency, is responsive to Canadian law and social policy and seeks to reflect policy in its programs and productions. Beginning in the 1960s in the context of Prime Minister Pierre Trudeau's liberal platform of a Canadian "participatory democracy," the NFB sought to equip disenfranchised social groups, including Indigenous people, with the film apparatus to produce their own representations with the idea that "media representation might effectively bring about improved political representation" (127).[10] This mission was reinvigorated in subsequent decades with increasing population and political shifts in Canada. From the 1980s onward, Canadian social policy was framed in terms of "diversity" to manage and govern population changes, including increased immigration, the Quebec sovereignty referendum of 1980, and Indigenous demands for autonomy (168). In response, the NFB prioritized youth, women, and minorities, and opened Studio I—the Indigenous studio—in 1991. Through Studio I, the NFB sought to provide institutional resources—including training, equipment and technology, and facilities—to equip Indigenous filmmakers to undertake their own projects. Owing to its programs and resources for representing Indigenous social realities, the NFB has been discussed as facilitating Indigenous cultural continuity. In "Studio One: Of Storytellers and Stories," Maria de Rosa (2002, 329–30) links NFB media practice with Indigenous cultural traditions, citing statements by Indigenous filmmakers, including Loretta Todd and Carol Geddes, who relate that filmmaking is a part of a continuum of "storytelling." De Rosa evokes a discourse of Indigenous media as an extension of Indigenous cultural tradition, which overlaps with the NFB's social empowerment mission. *Our World*'s design explicitly brings together cultural revitalization with social empowerment: "Before the projects are produced, we ask each community to identify young people interested in visual art and/or story-telling . . . We then send instructors to the First Nations communities where they spend a week working with a group of young people who then create their own short films in the First Nations' language. At the end of the week, a public screening of their work is held to celebrate their accomplishments and to invite the community to come see and hear the stories" (National Film Board of Canada 2011). The project thus engages with an urgent social issue, the decline in Indigenous language speakers, by seeking to equip Indigenous youth specifically with the media skills to develop projects to support language retention. In this configuration, film and media have a role to play in cultural continuity. However, *Cry Rock* reflects on the role of digital technology in transmitting Indigenous cultural knowledge, and what is changed, or even lost, when cultural knowledge is recorded. *Cry Rock* intervenes in prevailing discourses of media's relationship to Indigenous cultures, arguing that this dynamic risks conflating oral traditions with recording technologies. *Cry Rock* thereby enters into a critical dialogue with national cultural policy and institutional discourses that challenges their underpinning logics in order to create space to reflect on the specificities of oral traditions.

Visualizing Cultural Mediations

The pervasiveness of Western cultural influences on Indigenous communities is visually conveyed through the representation of a broad range of media technologies: notebooks, a reel-to-reel recorder, photographs, DVDs, and video cameras. The film is ambivalent about the use of these technologies, at once acknowledging that they play a role in cultural preservation while at the same time arguing for the distinctiveness and value of oral traditions. Hanuse's voice-over rhetorically enacts this ambivalence: it is structured as a series of questions about her reluctance to record her grandmother's stories and reflections on her childhood, bracketing her perspective to create a point of departure for representing others'. Hanuse's cousin, Deborah Nelson, is shown in the process of video-recording her father's stories so that she can both preserve them and learn from them. She is particularly interested in the more recent history of when the entire village was moved from the north side of the river to the south side due to a historic smallpox epidemic. She both records him at home speaking Nuxalk, and also travels with him to the old site of the river where the village once stood, recording her father's memories on a small digital camera. Nelson could be said to be using a "mixed mode" approach to oral history, in which electronic recording and oral narratives are both involved to record cultural knowledge. Hanuse, however, is interested

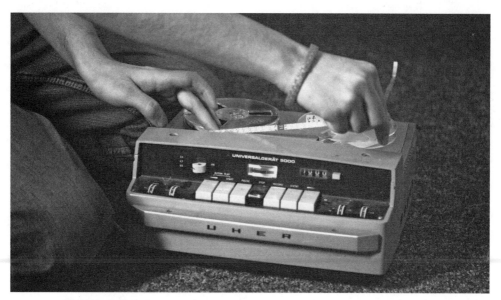

FIGURE 3. A still from *Cry Rock*. Snxakila (Clyde Tallio) loads reel-to-reel tape of Nuxalk language recording.

in the specificity and value of oral traditions. Though Nelson asserts that recording is imperative because every time an elder dies those stories are lost, Hanuse states in voice-over, "And still, when I turn my camera on my grandmother, I can't bring myself to ask her for her stories." Though Hanuse gives space to represent a perspective supporting the use of recording technologies, the film distinguishes the two in order to give oral traditions their due.

In addition to interviews with community members, the film features evocative watercolor animation of Hanuse's memories of her youth learning from elders in the community. These sequences are warm and intimate, and as Nuxalk is spoken, the words appear in watercolor on screen, conveying that the Nuxalk language is "animated" and alive in these environments. *Cry Rock* describes language and stories as living entities that are a part of the cultural history, and this cultural history lives within a physical and social world. In "Oral Tradition and Oral History: Reviewing Some Issues" Julie Cruikshank (1994) describes the unique social and historical character of oral narratives. Cruikshank, an anthropologist who has done extensive ethnographic work with Indigenous peoples to theorize oral traditions, evaluates prevailing analytic approaches to oral traditions: they have been considered material culture that give evidence of the past, and have been theorized as a method for interpreting and understanding social conditions in the present. To these dominant interpretive methods she adds more contemporary approaches that recognize that the meanings of oral narratives are not self-evident, but must be understood in social practice where meaning is enacted.

Context is particularly meaningful for oral histories because they bear an intrinsic relationship to place. Cruikshank cites a case study of an anthropologist conducting field research with Indigenous groups in the Philippines, in which he came to understand that in oral traditional modes, "events are anchored to place and people use locations in space to speak about events over time" (409). Thus, by relating events to place, oral narratives shape perception of the landscape as a part of history. Oral narratives resist codification—which would render them into a static form—because their meaning comes from the context of their telling, enacted by the person relating the narrative in a particular place where that narrative is "located."

Cry Rock explores dimensions of oral narratives that convey place relationships. The film crew travels with Clyde Tallio, a young Nuxalk speaker, and Alvin Mack, a local Nuxalk artist, to a site they believe might be the Cry Rock, a spot in a local river where, as Clyde describes, a supernatural being called the Sniniq once sat crying for her dead child. Two local boys heard her crying and approached her in their boat, and when one boy stepped out on the rock next to her, he began crying, too. After a while the Sniniq turned to him and thanked him for crying with her. Alvin's voice is heard over a long shot of the bend in the river that he believes could be the site of the story, and the camera slowly zooms in to consider the spot. The story is shown to have a physical and historical location and it transforms perceptions of the site; the story "becomes real" in the world, living in a particular territory. This scene

FIGURE 4. A still from *Cry Rock*. Alvin Mack and Snxakila (Clyde Tallio) at the site of the Cry Rock (Kwanatulhayc).

links storytelling to place, something the film can point to but cannot reproduce or embody.

The Sniniq story also tells another story, one about the limitations of electronic recordings to communicate the full meaning of oral narratives. The young boy who joins the Sniniq on the Cry Rock experiences her grief empathetically, but does not share the source of her grief. The Cry Rock becomes a site of mediation, where a certain social and cultural interaction can take place, but a fullness of understanding through shared experience is not realizable. It is telling that the Sniniq is a mother and the boy a child—in the story's telling in the film, they are from different generations. Generational difference is therefore the framework for the disjuncture between them, echoing the generational ruptures experienced within Indigenous communities. Elsewhere in the film, the presence and influence of the elementary school in the community is foregrounded, evoking the colonial education system and its impact on Indigenous communities and cultures. As Clyde Tallio relates, the provincial educational curriculum limits the amount of time that the Nuxalk language can be taught in class to thirty minutes a week—in effect, perpetuating the colonial project of cultural erosion through its inadequate language programming.

The relationship between the boy and the Sniniq allegorizes Hanuse's own relationship with her grandmother. Like the boy, she is at a remove from her grandmother's conceptual and cultural frameworks by virtue of descending from a generation in which a profound cultural disruption took place. Her relationship with her grandmother is therefore mediated by a generational cultural shift. This should not, however, be understood as an inflexible barrier to understanding. Though Indigenous communities have experienced an irrevocable cultural change over the past several centuries, Julie Cruikshank helps us to understand that oral traditions are used to make sense of contemporary circumstances, and gain meaning in practice as they relate to those circumstances. Oral narratives are thus flexible and adaptive, constantly making sense of the present in particular places. As illustrated by the film, the Cry Rock story allegorizes the generational rupture, and reflects on the cultural and social changes that have taken place in the community as a result. It simultaneously identifies the limitations the documentary mode, since we cannot be in the physical place to which the story refers and in which it is meaningful. The film thus argues that oral narratives are able to account for cultural and historical change—and in fact, are meaningful in that they do address the present—while at the same time requiring certain conditions in order to be more fully meaningful: the language in which they are relayed and the environment in which they live. Oral traditions are both flexible and finite, and the film registers this tension, particularly since the conditions through which these stories are meaningful are increasingly under threat. Though different conceptual frameworks will be at play due to generational differences, the film makes the case that given the right conditions, the knowledge that the stories possess can be transmitted across that divide.

As in *Navajo Talking Picture,* the representation of Hanuse's relationship with her grandmother is a central trope of the film. Whereas the conflict-based interactions between Bowman and Ann Biah thematized cultural conflict as the structuring device of the film, Hanuse and her grandmother do not interact on camera for the majority of the film; rather, her grandmother appears in a sequence in which she prepares and smokes a salmon, which is intercut throughout the film and which the camera observes discreetly. I would argue that it functions pedagogically, modeling a kind of careful attentiveness required in oral traditions. The camera is aligned with Hanuse's perspective, enhanced by the film's first-person narration and Hanuse's memories. While her grandmother prepares the salmon, the camera-as-Hanuse patiently observes. While the film ultimately argues that oral traditions cannot be fully realized through the film apparatus, it guides the viewer toward recognition of the interpersonal dynamics necessary to participate in them. At the end of the film, Hanuse states that she decided to learn the Nuxalk stories following the oral tradition, and in a long shot she runs from behind the camera up to her grandmother's porch steps to embrace her. This shot

FIGURE 5. A still from *Cry Rock*. Anuximana (Violet Tallio) bagging salmon (slaq'k).

complements the salmon preparation sequence in that it suggests that attentiveness, modeled throughout the film, has prepared her for the interpersonal relationships required of oral traditions.

Cry Rock's intervention is particularly timely given the proliferation of Indigenous film and media production worldwide. The film's attention to the value and relevance of oral traditions and critique of the applications and limitations of recording technologies is crucial ballast for social and institutional discourses that align media with oral traditions. It thus brings together critical frameworks from Indigenous studies with discourses around Indigenous production from state-sponsored film institutions. Attention to the institutional dimensions of the film illuminates an area of discursive convergence that enables a productive critique of discourses conflating filmmaking with oral traditions, enabling closer examination of these two modes and their specificities.

Conclusion

In a sense, the insights of both *Navajo Talking Picture* and *Cry Rock* pivot around the limits of representation. *Navajo Talking Picture* shows the audience Bowman's "failure," which demarcates the boundary of what she sought to represent—her grandmother's traditional lifestyle—and what she is unable to, which is ultimately attributed to the irreconcilability of their cultural positions. *Cry Rock,* meanwhile, shows the audience what it cannot show, since the film apparatus, and indeed any other recording technology, cannot represent the fuller meaning of oral traditional narratives.

Though produced in different national contexts, both *Navajo Talking Picture* and *Cry Rock* emerge in relation to university programs affiliated with Indigenous studies, and their films give evidence of their negotiations with institutional discourses and practices in their production and ultimately in their screen content. At UCLA, the "reinvention" anthropology sought to involve Indigenous people in the production and interpretation of research, but did not anticipate or understand how colonial processes might be replicated in what was intended to be a culturally empowering project. In trying to better represent Indigenous needs, the NFB designed programming to support Indigenous social empowerment that aligned Indigenous media with traditional cultural practices, perhaps not fully cognizant that even with the best of intentions contemporary applications of media for engaging with Indigenous cultural knowledge risk displacing traditional modalities. These films do, however, make visible the complexities arising out of such efforts and contribute to understandings of the possibilities and limitations of particular institutional approaches, valuable insights that can advance institutional and disciplinary practices in Indigenous studies and other studies of marginalized groups.

Attention to institutional contexts adds nuance and complexity to the interpretation of Indigenous production, opening up further areas of study for Indigenous media as social phenomenon. While institutions such as state cultural agencies and postsecondary programs do not dictate or control Indigenous production, Indigenous filmmakers navigate their representational practices and funding structures in the production of their work, which demonstrates complex engagement with prevailing discourses of Indigeneity and cultural representation. Far from replicating their terms, these filmmakers complicate and challenge them, indicating that these films are as much a source of theory of Indigenous representation as the scholarship surrounding them, and should be understood as such.

KARRMEN CREY (Sto:lo) received her PhD in cinema and media studies from the University of California, Los Angeles.

Bibliography

Bowman, A. 1983. *Annual Report: Fiscal Year 1982–1983*. Los Angeles: UCLA American Indian Studies Center.

———. 1985. *Annual Report: Fiscal Year 1984–1985*. Los Angeles: UCLA American Indian Studies Center.

———. 1986. *Navajo Talking Picture*. New York: Women Make Movies.

———. 2015a. Interview with Karrmen Crey. July 7.

———. 2015b. E-mail to Karrmen Crey. October 31.

———. 2015c. Interview with Karrmen Crey. September 9.

Cook-Lynn, E. 1997. "Who Stole Native American Studies?" *Wicazo Sa Review* 12, no. 1: 9–28.

Cruikshank, J. 1994 "Oral Tradition and Oral History: Reviewing Some Issues." *Canadian Historical Review* 75, no. 3: 403–21.

Csordas, T. J. 1999. "Ritual Healing and the Politics of Identity in Contemporary Navajo Society." *American Ethnologist* 26, no. 1: 3–23.

De Rosa, M. 2002. "Studio One: Of Storytellers and Stories." In *North of Everything: English-Canadian Cinema since 1980,* eds. William Beard and Jerry White, 328–41. Edmonton: University of Alberta Press.

Dowell, K. L. 2013. *Sovereign Screens: Aboriginal Media on the Canadian West Coast*. Lincoln: University of Nebraska Press.

Druick, Z. 2007. *Projecting Canada: Government Policy and Documentary Film at the National Film Board*. Montreal: McGill-Queen's University Press.

Faris, J. C. 1996. *Navajo and Photography: A Critical History of the Representation of an American People*. Albuquerque: University of New Mexico Press.

First Nations Studies Program. n.d. "First Nations Studies at UBC." http://fnis.arts.ubc.ca/roots-of-fnsp/.

Ginsburg, F. 1991. "Indigenous Media: Faustian Contract or Global Village?" *Cultural Anthropology* 6, no. 1: 92–112.

———. 1994. "Embedded Aesthetics: Creating a Discursive Space for Indigenous Media." *Cultural Anthropology* 9, no. 3: 365–82.

———. 1995. "The Parallax Effect: The Impact of Aboriginal Media on Ethnographic Film." *Anthropology Review* 11, no. 2: 64–76.

Hafsteinsson, S. B. 2008. "Unmasking Deep Democracy: Aboriginal Peoples Television Network (APTN) and Cultural Production." Ph.D. diss., Temple University.

Hanson, E. 2009. "The Residential School System." *Indigenous Foundations*. http://indigenousfoundations.arts.ubc.ca.

Hanuse, B. 2010. *Cry Rock*. Smayaykila Films.

———. 2015. E-mail interview. April 14.

Hawkins, R. C. 1970. *Report of UCLA Ethnographic Film Project Funded in 1966 by CICS*. Los Angeles: UCLA Archives.

Hearne, J. 2012. *Native Recognition: Indigenous Cinema and the Western*. Albany, N.Y.: SUNY Press.

Hjort, M. 2013. "Introduction: More Than Film School—Why the Full Spectrum of Practice-Based Film Education Warrants Attention." In *The Education of the Filmmaker in Africa, the Middle East, and the Americas*, ed. M. Hjort, 1–22. New York: Palgrave Macmillan.

James, D. E. 2005. *The Most Typical Avant-Garde: History and Geography of Minor Cinemas in Los Angeles*. Berkeley: University of California Press.

Kesler, L. 2003a. "FNSP 310: Theory Seminar." University of British Columbia.

———. 2003b. "FNSP 320: Research Methods." University of British Columbia.

Lewis, R. 2012. *Navajo Talking Picture: Cinema on Native Ground*. Lincoln: University of Nebraska Press.

Limbrick, P. 2010. *Making Settler Cinemas: Film and Colonial Encounters in the United States, Australia, and New Zealand*. New York: Palgrave Macmillan.

Mamber, S. 1972. "Cinema-Verite in America: Part II—Direct Cinema and the Crisis Structure." *Screen* 13, no. 3: 114–36.

Mander, J. 1992. *In the Absence of the Sacred: The Failure of Technology and the Survival of the Indian Nations*. San Francisco: Sierra Club Books.

Marr, C. J. n.d. "Assimilation through Education." *American Indians of the Pacific Northwest Collection*. http://content.lib.washington.edu/aipnw/marr.html #movement.

Mather, E. 1995. "With a Vision Beyond Our Immediate Needs: Oral Traditions in an Age of Literacy." In *When Our Words Return: Writing, Reading, and Remembering Oral Traditions from Alaska and the Yukon*, eds. P. Morrow and W. Schneider, 13–26. Boulder, Colo.: Utah State University Press, University Press of Colorado.

Michaels, E. 1994. *Bad Aboriginal Art: Tradition, Media, and Technological Horizons*. Minneapolis: University of Minnesota Press.

National Film Board of Canada. 2011. "Our World." *National Film Board of Canada*. https://www.nfb.ca.

Noriega, Chon A. 2000. *Shot in America: Television, the State, and the Rise of Chicano Cinema*. Minneapolis: University of Minnesota Press.

Okada, Jun. 2015. *Making Asian American Film and Video: History, Institutions, Movements*. New Brunswick, N.J.: Rutgers University Press.

Pack, S. 2007. "Watching Navajos Watch Themselves." *Wicazo Sa Review* 22, no. 2: 111–27.

Petrie, D. 2010. "Theory, Practice, and the Significance of Film Schools." *Scandia* 76, no. 2: 31–46.

Singer, B. R. 2001. *Wiping the War Paint off the Lens: Native American Film and Video*. Minneapolis: University of Minnesota Press.

Smith, L. T. 1999. *Decolonizing Methodologies: Research and Indigenous Peoples*. London: Zed Books.

Tsinhnahjinnie, H. J. 1998. "When Is a Photograph Worth a Thousand Words?" http://www.hulleah.com.

Turner, T. 1992. "Defiant Images: The Kayapo Appropriation of Video." *Anthropology Today* 8, no. 6: 5–16.

UCLA American Indian Studies Center. 1980. *Five Year Report, 1975–1980*. Los Angeles: UCLA American Indian Studies Center.

Waugh, T., E. Winton, and M. B. Baker, eds. 2010. *Challenge for Change: Activist Documentary at the National Film Board of Canada*. Montreal: McGill-Queen's University Press.

Worth, S., and J. Adair. 1972. *Through Navajo Eyes: An Exploration in Film Communication and Anthropology*. Bloomington: Indiana University Press.

Notes

I would like to express my gratitude to Chon Noriega, Andrew deWaard, Alice Royer, Bryan Wuest, and Andrew Young, as well as to the anonymous reviewers and copyeditor, for reading versions of this article and for their generous comments and support.

1. Carolyn J. Marr (n.d.) provides an invaluable overview of the boarding school system in the United States. Erin Hanson (2009) provides a concise summary of the history and effects of the residential school system in Canada.

2. FNSP has since been renamed First Nations and Indigenous Studies. To remain consistent with research materials and interviews, I use FNSP throughout.

3. In *Navajo Talking Picture*, Bowman refers to herself as Diné, the traditional name of the Navajo people, though she often uses "Navajo" interchangeably. To remain consistent, I use "Diné" throughout this article except when quoting from the film or sources.

4. The "Navajo Long Walk" refers to the period of the 1860s when the Diné people were removed from their traditional territories by the U.S. government and made to march to eastern New Mexico, where they were forcibly resettled. Thousands died during and as a consequence of the march and resettlement, a collective trauma that Thomas J. Csordas (1999, 4) has argued "is critical to contemporary Navajos' sense of identity as a people."

5. Perhaps most widely known is Sol Worth and James Adair's Navajo Film Project, an anthropological endeavor that sought to discover a Diné worldview by equipping Diné community members with film cameras to shoot their own

short documentaries. The results were more telling of the anthropologists' assumptions about Indigenous culture, authenticity, and documentary verisimilitude, and the project has subsequently become a touchstone for debates about Indigenous self-representation and the mediating effects of the cinematic apparatus. See Worth and Adair (1972).

6. Terence Turner (1992) and Joanna Hearne (2012) have critiqued Faris for his claims that the film and photographic apparatuses are inherently colonial because they construct their subjects always as "the Other." They argue that this position denies the agency of Indigenous filmmakers, and overlooks the specific social relations that Indigenous viewers may have with the images, relations that the Taskigi/Diné artist Hulleah J. Tsinhnahjinnie theorizes in terms of "photographic sovereignty," which describes Indigenous reinterpretation of Indigenous images. Sam Pack's (2007) ethnographic work of Diné audiences' responses to film and television representations of Diné people can also be understood in terms of Indigenous reception studies.

7. While these emphases center Indigenous knowledge and experiences, Indigenous studies is, and has always been, an interdisciplinary field with a wide range of Indigenous and non-Indigenous specialists.

8. Faye Ginsburg (1995) provides a concise summary of this epistemological shift in light of political movements of colonized peoples beginning in the 1960s onward, and Indigenous people's increased participation in self-authored media.

9. Snapshots of the "Our World" website were located through the Internet Archive Wayback Machine (http://archive.org/web/), which do not retain its full content, an unfortunate reality of the ephemerality of Internet-based records.

10. Called "Challenge for Change," this activist documentary initiative has been widely discussed, and has received extensive examination in Waugh, Winton, and Baker (2010).

MARY CAPPELLI

Innovative Strategies of Indigenous Resistance among the Wounaan People of Colombia

THE WOUNAAN PEOPLE of northwestern Colombia's San Juan River are the latest casualty of a violent twenty-five-year reign of terror hastened by the convergence of coca growers, gold miners, paramilitaries, guerillas, and government troops—all vying for control of the waterways and resources along the ancestral stretch of traditional Wounaan territories.[1] Until the arrival of mono-crop production for export, Wounaan's steadfast strategies have thwarted the bloodied battlefields of Spanish colonial impositions, nationalist armies, and Marxist guerrillas. Occupying small thatched huts stilted on posts hovering up to eight feet high along the clearings on the riverbanks, the Wounaan kept to their subsistence livelihoods of hunting, fishing, Werregue Palm basket-weaving, and small-scale agriculture of bananas, pineapples, and yucca. That is until November 2014, when the Wounaan people were forced to leave their village of Unión Aguas Claras along the San Juan River of the Cauca Valley and take up a twelve-month residence in El Cristal Sports Arena in Buenaventura, Colombia.

According to Wounaan spokesman Crelo Obispo, "Paramilitaries kicked us out of land," and for twelve months they worked diligently to "find a peaceful way to recover our own indigenous land."[2] The Wounaan turned their occupation into a form of civil disobedience and refused to return to their lands without adequate protection and security from warring factions. Although on November 29, 2015, they returned home along the San Juan River, their cultural survival signals a critical humanitarian and environmental emergency in which Indigenous people living sustainable lives have been caught in a resource war for coca cultivation, gold mining, and control of key river tributaries. As an interdisciplinary ethnographer and witness for peace, I had the opportunity to accompany the Wounaan in their occupation of El Cristal and to make visible the distinctive resistance tactics they employed to defend their right to living in their native territories.[3]

Occupy El Cristal

For a full year, 343 Wounaan people, 63 families, occupied the cold hard floor of the basketball courts, sleeping in multicolored, handwoven hammocks strung beneath the stadium bleachers. One of them was a young wearied mother holding a shirtless eleven-month-old infant suffering from a burning fever and bouts of diarrhea and vomiting. She recalled, "There wasn't any medicine."[4] Herein lies the crisis. Not only were mothers unable to gain access to traditional herbal medicines, they were also unable to gain access to modern health care. Three somber mothers told me they were running out of adequate food and water sources. Buenaventura officials confirmed the death of two young children, one-year-old Neiber Cárdenas Pirza in December 2014 and a two-day-old baby in June 2014. The Wounaan claimed the deaths were a result of inadequate health care and living conditions in the sports arena. "Our people practice culture, artistry, spirituality and traditional medicine. We need our lands to do so," said Obispo.[5]

The affirmative belief that the Wounaan were "occupying" the sports arena and taking a political stand against their dispossession by violence is key to understanding Wounaan resistance. "We arrived November 28, 2014, and since that time we had been in resistance," Chama Puto said.[6] Because "the local government hardly did anything, and gave no guarantees of assistance," he urgently called on international help and social advocacy networks to "get meetings with entities who could make change" and affirmed Wounaan ancestral ties to their lands. "Land doesn't belong to the government or police. It belongs to the indigenous," he added.[7]

Although Wounaan Leaders such as Chama Puto are well versed in Colombia's constitutional law, they are fully aware of how constitutional decrees have remained rhetorical discourses because of the government's failure to implement constitutional protections within its infrastructure—an absence of institutional support that has undermined the visionary purpose of the protections. In particular, Article 63 states, "Communal lands of ethnic groups and reservation lands cannot be taken away or attached";[8] Article 72 states, "Ethnic groups settled in areas of archeological treasures have special rights over that cultural heritage, which rights must be regulated by law";[9] Article 246 provides that "the authorities of the indigenous peoples may exercise jurisdictional functions within their territories, in accordance with their own standards and procedures, provided they do not conflict with the Constitution and laws of the Republic."[10]

While in some cases legal maneuvering and mobilization within Colombian courts have served to defend Indigenous landholdings, the yearlong Wounaan occupation of El Cristal is a blatant recognition of the ineffectiveness of Colombia's legislation and juridical processes. Innovative forms of resistance appeal to wider sociopolitical networks capable of eliciting support across local, regional, national, and global borders; however, it comes with a price.

Rhizomic World

El Cristal Sports Arena is a far cry from the Wounaan's rhizomic world of heterogeneity and its interconnected relations of all plant, animal, ancestral, and human life living within its ecosystems. This dynamic cartography of interconnected networks mapped across their ancestral rhizomic river systems and landscape moves beyond Western metaphysical notions of duality to foster a cosmos of inter-being. For the Wounaan, the San Juan River is an essential organizing principle of their rhizomic networking system, rich in its biodiversity, in which their cosmology interconnects them to 8,000–9,000 vascular plants, 577 bird species, 52 snake species, 45 lizard and allied species, and 127 amphibian species—all inter-being in an ecosystem without hierarchies. In addition to its cohesive social networks, the San Juan River is the true river (*döchaar*) and ancestral homeland, and thus a material feature in the development of their worldview and their perceptions of themselves.[11]

Wounaan livelihood and well-being rely on their interaction with their landscape, an animistic, ethno-geographic interaction grounded in rhizomic thought in which "any point of a rhizome can be connected to anything other, and must be."[12] These beliefs further their kinship networks across time and space in a continuous state of growth in which identities and relationships extend and merge through a web of intersecting relationships. Bill Ashcroft explains the rhizome in biological imagery as a multiplying "root system which spreads across the ground" from varying points, reaching out across the nomadic space "rather than a single tap root."[13]

The fluvial systems crisscross over a three-dimensional topography, which includes portals to the underworld, the real world, and the celestial world. In this way their river-dominated cosmos reflects the comings and goings on the river up (*marag*), down (*badag*), to (*jerag*), and from (*durrag*) in a world where spirits, beings, plants, and animals in the visible and invisible world live in a balance of reciprocal equilibrium.[14]

Because of their metaphysical approach, which links native individualities, political strategies, and traditional subsistence practices, they have been able to maintain their traditional livelihoods and ways of being against the onslaught of land dispossession and acculturation.[15] Although their rhizomic community is resistant to rupture where it has fissured and people are de-territorialized, the river's organic networking systems have been capable of reattaching the Wounaan to people, plants, and animals within its extended network or creating new connections across its geographical space.[16]

Since the 1990s, the San Juan River's fluvial systems have been become destabilized spaces in which flows of capital, commodities, and contraband have brought in a host of nonlocal actors vying for spatial control of its strategic geographies. These vital commercial river networks, which connect the Colombian interior with the Pacific Coast, are needed for the production and transportation of gold mining excavation and cocoa cultivation, turning the once-peaceful rhizomic ecosystem into a bloody battleground between narco traffickers, gold miners, FARC, the ELN, the Urabeños, the Rastrojos, and other left-wing, right-wing, and neo-paramilitary forces.

The result is not only the displacement of Indigenous peoples and the disruption of the natural equilibrium of the Wounaan subsistent lifestyle, but the destruction of the biodiverse habitat in which its diverse resources have been transformed to commercial assets and mobilized for mono-crop and gold production of surplus value. Added to the actors competing for resources is the introduction of new players from the National Development Plan hoping to position the San Juan River as a key geographic territory for the neoliberal exploitation of resources for free trade agreements. More important, dispossession for capitalist production has led to the desecration of ancestral homelands in which families are increasingly intimidated, disappeared, and butchered by a collusion of local and nonlocal actors to expedite commodity commerce.

"The government said we are something in the way of development," said Crelo Obispo, further noting, "We've been attacked by our conqueror."[17] Another Wounaan spokesman added, "They want to exterminate us."[18] Whether it is death by paramilitary, death by narco trafficker, or death in the crossfire between guerillas and the army, there is one certainty as Crelo Obispo declares: return to their homeland is precarious and must be "met with protection and dignity."[19]

Amid these conditions are ongoing negotiations for a bilateral ceasefire between the government and FARC. Although the Colombian government and FARC rebels have moved toward a comprehensive plan to end an ongoing civil war which, since 1964, has killed 220,000 people, the Wounaan have still been left out in the cold.[20] Chama Puto points out that while they are negotiating in Havana, Cuba, "we had been ignored in all negotiation processes."[21] He believes that conflict resolution can result only when "the government negotiates with all its people."[22]

As of today this has not happened, and the people the color of the soil, who turned their displacement into a political strategy of Indigenous resistance to the destruction of their traditional ecosystems, still struggle for survival. Chama Puto wants a governmental guarantee of protection and safety in order to survive on their ancestral lands. "We are done negotiating," he said.[23]

Forceful dispossession underpins the plight of the Wounaan whose homeland has been drained by capital's international reach for resources, in which a "free market exchange relies on and takes advantage of the political and cultural dispossession of certain subjects."[24] How do Indigenous people who make up 2 percent of Colombia's population coexist in a global world that renders them disposable, inhuman beings? In this scenario, the 2 percent making up the Indigenous groups of Colombia become 8 percent of the dispossessed, displaced, destined to misery as a form of "human waste"—sadly, a myth narrated and played out in the many parts of the globe.

In El Cristal, the Wounaan were separated from their means of subsistence and vigorously resisted all paradigms of commercial expansion and regional control of their economies—a pattern in which "more than 5.7 million people have been internally displaced in Colombia since the start of recording official cumulative registration figures."[25] As of 2014, Colombia's National Victims' Unit documented 97,453 cases of forced displacement, mostly in the Pacific region. The El Cristal crisis exposed the systematic layers of political collusion that render Wounaan territories disposable sites of exploitation and economic casualties, which dispossess its peoples from their traditional livelihoods for the benefit of regional, national, and global markets.

Wounaan Resistance Strategies

Wounaan resistance strategies date back to colonization and manifested in the traditional tactics they implemented to maintain their sense of cultural dignity during their resistance campaign. While living in the sports arena, women practiced small-scale *artesanías* in the form of colorful bracelets, necklaces, earrings, and carved wooden bowls. The unbroken practice of these customs created communal solidarity and furthered their economic livelihoods, traditional knowledge, and cultural sustainability. Although these courageous women were proud to sell their crafts to sports arena visitors, the transactions were soured by the reality of their dispossession. "Collectively and physically the living conditions" were "inadequate, the food inadequate."[26]

Wounaan resilience to reattach itself to its rhizomic rivers network is precarious and subject to intra-institutional support of regional and national control. It has yet to be seen whether this latest mobilization strategy will provide any safeguards and protections for their community. "Promises have been unfulfilled and we have become strangers to ourselves," sighed a wearied Obispo.[27]

MARY CAPPELLI is a graduate and interdisciplinary scholar from USC, UCLA, and Loyola Law School, where she studied anthropology; theater, film, and television; and law and literature. A former lecturer at Emerson College, she is a member of the National Indigenous Women's Resource Center and researches the impact of globalization on Indigenous populations in Africa and Central America.

Notes

1. Agro-industrial mono-cultivation of sugar, maize, palm oil, and soybean, powered by the demand for biofuels from the global North, has displaced populations and ecosystems throughout Colombia. For more information on how the industrialized North pushes developing countries to monoculture see the December 12, 2011, Social Watch report, "Industrialized North Drives Developing Countries to Monoculture," http://www.socialwatch.org/.

2. Chama Puto, interview by author, tape recording, Buenaventura, Colombia, September 6, 2014.

3. My ethnographic approach to understanding the Wounaan community consisted of a qualitative approach of collecting secondary data analysis, including archival legal data from local, regional, and national offices beginning in December 2014 and extending until October 2015. In September 2014 I observed living conditions and activities within El Cristal, recorded field notes, and conducted informal and semi-structured interviews. I observed that while the community was extremely exhausted and frustrated, they never lost hope of their goal of returning home.

4. Wounaan mother, interview by author, tape recording, Buenaventura, Colombia, September 6, 2014.

5. Crelo Obispo, interview by author, tape recording, Buenaventura, Colombia, September 6, 2014.

6. Puto interview, September 6.

7. Ibid.

8. *Colombia's Constitution of 1991 with Amendments through 2005* (Oxford, U.K.: Oxford University Press, 2016), Art. 63, p. 17.

9. Ibid., Art. 72, p. 19.

10. Ibid., Art. 246, p. 68.

11. Julie Velásquez Runk, "And the Creator Began to Carve Us of Cocobolo: Culture, History, Forest Ecology, and Conservation among Wounaan in Eastern Panama" (Ph.D. diss., Yale University, 2005).

12. Gilles Deleuze and Felix Guattari, *A Thousand Plateaus: Capitalism and Schizophrenia* (Minneapolis: University of Minnesota Press, 2007), 7

13. Bill Ashcroft, "The Rhizome of Post-Colonial Discourse," in *Literature and the Contemporary: Fictions and Theories of the Present,* ed. Roger Luckhurst and Peter Marks (London: Longman, 1999), 116.

14. Velásquez Runk, "And the Creator Began to Carve Us of Cocobolo."

15. Marcela Velasco. "Contested Territoriality: Ethnic Challenges to Colombia's Territorial Regimes," *Bulletin of Latin American Research* 30, no. 2 (2011): 214.

16. Zena Kamash, "What Lies Beneath? Perceptions of the Ontological Paradox of Water," *World Archeology* 40, no. 2 (2008): 224–37.

17. Crelo Obispo, interview by author, tape recording, Buenaventura, Colombia, September 7, 2014.

18. Group interview by author, tape recording, Buenaventura, Colombia, September 7, 2014.

19. Obispo interview, September 7.

20. Sibylla Brodzinsky, "Colombia's Government and FARC Rebels Reach Agreement in Step to End Civil War," *The Guardian,* December 15, 2015.

21. Puto interview, September 6.

22. Ibid.

23. Ibid.

24. Rosemary Hennessy, *Fires on the Border: The Passionate Politics of Labor Organizing on the Mexican Frontera* (Minneapolis: University of Minnesota Press, 2013), 142.

25. The UN Refugee Agency, "2015 UNHCR Country Operations Profile: Colombia," http://www.unhcr.org/.

26. Wounaan mother interview, September 6.

27. Obispo interview, September 7.

JESSICA LANDAU

Edgar Heap of Birds
by Bill Anthes
Duke University Press, 2015

BILL ANTHES'S MONOGRAPH on contemporary artist Edgar Heap of Birds is as subversive as the artist's work. Anthes writes that his initial impulse was to use this text to insert Heap of Birds, a Cheyenne and Arapaho artist, into the American canon, a place where American Indian artists are frequently ignored. The book instead delves into a deeper understanding of Heap of Birds's work, grounded in a Cheyenne cosmology, while also beginning to challenge and deconstruct the art historical reliance on the canon at all. Through nonlinear readings of Heap of Birds's oeuvre, Anthes's richly illustrated text begins to take to heart Heap of Birds's challenge to the writing of history, illuminating the moments in which the artworks themselves write their own histories.

From the start, the book refuses the typical art historical model and does not follow a simple timeline of the artist's career. Instead, Anthes organizes chapters by themes, and allows the works themselves to create their own chronology. For example, early on he references Heap of Birds's *Neuf* paintings, a series of abstracted landscapes, which come up again and again in relation to his other works, letting the art historical narrative spiral in on itself. His four chapters—"Land," "Words," "Histories," and "Generations"— are not only directly relevant to the artworks discussed, but are representative of the number four, an important number in Cheyenne epistemology and particularly in the Earth Renewal Ceremony, as well as a direct reference to the *Neuf* series (*neuf* is four in Cheyenne). In this way, Anthes contextualizes Heap of Birds simultaneously in the international contemporary art world (comparing him to postmodernists and those who worked in the identity politics movement of the 1990s) while also grounding him firmly in Cheyenne tradition.

While the book is divided into these four thematic chapters, it does not follow a typical chronology or limit any of Heap of Birds's work to solely one category. By following this thematic structure, or rather spiral, Anthes demonstrates the interconnectivity of Heap of Birds's work through time and space, as well as its connections to the works it references, influences, or those that preempted it. Anthes returns to earlier-discussed works, not in a repetitive fashion, but in a mode that reveals their complexity and the depth of research Heap of Birds undertakes so frequently in his process.

Anthes's text is equally well researched—his discussion of individual artworks frequently delves into historical analysis. Again, this interest in history allows the author to spiral beyond the context of the artworks themselves, instead focusing on the broader histories and spaces the works function within as well as create. In a sense, then, the book models itself after Heap of Birds's own practice, using meticulous research and wit to gesture to the power of the symbolic and unearth the voices that history has attempted to suppress.

While it is nearly impossible to dislodge the form of the scholarly monograph completely without falling into illegible, Dada-like absurdity, Anthes presents a text that respects multiple traditions while directly refuting hegemonic colonial systems, like Enlightenment chronologies and the violent histories of naming and claiming. As a white art historian myself, I believe Anthes provides a good model of sensitive historical research, artist interviews, as well as formal analysis and art historical comparison to highlight the importance of Edgar Heap of Birds and his sovereignty in the contemporary art world while never denying or tokenizing his Indigeneity. While he set out to insert Heap of Birds into the postmodern canon, Anthes's text does more to challenge our reliance on the canon, at the very least, and perhaps even calls for its eradication.

Through his artwork Heap of Birds frequently asks viewers, "Who owns history?" Instead of attempting to answer this question, Anthes illuminates the importance of asking it, and perhaps suggests that he is not the one to answer such questions, suggesting instead that the artworks themselves will continue this cycle of questioning into future generations.

JESSICA LANDAU is a PhD student in art history at the University of Illinois at Urbana—Champaign.

GREG OLSON

Chenoo
by Joseph Bruchac
University of Oklahoma Press, 2016

"**THE PAST,** like the roots of a tree, holds up the present. Trace those roots and you may find the source of whatever it is that is going on now, especially when some of those roots turn out to be rotten" (109). These are the reflections of Penacook private investigator Jacob "Podjo" Neptune. As the book opens, Podjo's cousin Dennis Mitchell calls the smart-aleck P.I., who is a student of martial arts, keeper of Abenaki oral tradition, dispenser of Native humor and part-time poet, to investigate two grisly murders on Abenaki Island, his people's ancestral home.

The investigation, however, is complicated by the horrific nature of the crimes and events that are unfolding on the island. A group of intertribal activists, who call themselves the Children of the Mountain, have taken over a state campground located on land that rightfully belongs to the Abenakis. Their intention is to protect the land not only from the federal government but also from those in their own tribal government who would develop it into a casino and resort. During the siege, two of the occupiers are brutally attacked and killed (one victim even appears to have been partially devoured) by what investigators can only guess is a bear or possibly a wicked Chenoo, or Windigo.

Despite the classic setup, *Chenoo* is far from your typical whodunit. As author Joseph Bruchac makes clear in his preface, the novel is "about Native American rights, about the power of tradition and story [and] about martial arts" (v). To this I would add that *Chenoo* is also about time and memory and our various cultural attitudes about them. As Podjo and his cousin Dennis evade police blockades to assist the activists, many of whom they had grown up with years earlier, they rely on each of these vital elements to help lead them to the killer or killers.

While Podjo's practice of martial arts allows him to survive predicaments in which he is physically outnumbered or outmatched, it is his awareness of tradition and cultural memory that guides him throughout the book. While on the trail of the killer, he often recalls centuries-old oral traditions that relate to the challenges he faces. In this way, both author and protagonist remind us that "stories count" and can be useful resources for guiding us through life (ix). Stories also help Podjo size up those around him. In one instance, he chalks up his unease with a character named Mook to old stories that recount how Mook's family descended from toads.

Dreams, too, play an important role in Podjo's investigation. Foes fought in his vivid nightmares prepare him to take on adversaries in real life. In another scene, a dream remembered from days earlier leads him to the body of a victim who had been attacked but survives.

Even the land is an ally in the investigation as Dennis and Pudjo take comfort in the fact that they are protected by their ancestral home. They are confident that any outsiders who dare to attack them there will be at a dual disadvantage of being both unfamiliar with the land and unloved by it.

I find Bruchac's use of time and memory to be one of the novel's most fascinating elements. Throughout Podjo's adventures, he utilizes the habits and knowledge of long-dead Abenaki warriors who are never far away. "As we stand on this hilltop we call the present moment," Podjo muses, "most of us look only at the ground just before our feet. Some of us, blessed or cursed with longer sight, lift our eyes to discern what lies ahead . . . or turn our heads to look farther back. Then we must be prepared for what we see" (129).

This brings us finally to the central metaphor of the book, the Chenoo or Windigo monster found throughout Algonquin oral tradition. At various points, Bruchac compares the monster to the federal government, land developers, and those who lust for positions of power. Because the Chenoo was once a human who was turned into a terrible creature by its own insatiable greed, it reminds us now, as it has for centuries, of the dangers of our own desires. In this tale, Bruchac has succeeded in making time circle back by engaging readers with a story as old as the Chenoo itself.

GREG OLSON is Curator of Exhibits and Special Projects at the Missouri State Archives.

BEENASH JAFRI

Alien Capital: Asian Racialization and the Logic of Settler Colonial Capitalism
   by Iyko Day
Duke University Press, 2016

IN *ALIEN CAPITAL*, Iyko Day offers readers insightful, intersectional cultural criticism that examines how Asian American and Asian Canadian literary and visual cultures expose and rupture settler-colonial capitalist logics. Joining a growing body of literature that complicates the Native/settler binary framing settler-colonial studies, Day develops a model for understanding settler-colonialism that is triangulated through white, Indigenous, and "alien" subject positions. The alien refers to the racialized migrant on whose labor settler capitalism relies. Like Glen Coulthard's *Red Skin, White Masks,* which draws attention to how settler-colonialism is constitutive of capitalism in the United States and Canada, Day hones in on the settler-colonial organization of racial capitalism in North America, where Indigenous claims to land and an ongoing demand for labor shape the contours of capitalist production. *Alien Capital* is particularly concerned with romantic anticapitalism as a key dimension of settler-colonial logic. Romantic anticapitalism refers to the conflation of capitalism with the objects capitalism fetishizes (for example, machines). Within romantic anticapitalist discourses, Asian bodies, due to their perceived hyper-efficiency, come to signify the evils of capitalism. This leads Day to argue that capitalism does not merely obscure—or make abstract—the concrete relations of race, gender, and sexuality through which it is characterized, but that this abstraction is constituted *through* the racialization of the Asian body.

   Alien Capital consists of an introduction, four chapters, and an epilogue. In concise and elegant prose, each chapter analyzes two Asian diasporic literary or visual texts, one American and Canadian. Day's methodology for studying Asian North America is transnational—not merely comparative—with settler-colonial capitalism as the bridging frame. As she outlines in the introduction, Day's interpretations of the cultural texts foreground their white settler-colonial capitalist contexts. Her careful readings show how these cultural productions expose and challenge a central feature of settler capitalist logics: namely, that Asians embody the abstraction of capitalism. In chapter 1, Day analyzes Richard Fung's experimental video documentary *Dirty Laundry* alongside Maxine Hong Kingston's "The Grandfather of the Sierra Nevada Mountains," from her experimental memoir *China Men.* Her focus here is on how these two texts queerly disrupt the linear constructions of time and national history—constitutive of settler capitalism—that position

Asians as efficient in their use of labor-time. Turning to the visual art of Tseng Kwong Chi and Jin-Me Yoon, the second chapter draws on the late José Esteban Muñoz's theory of disidentification to examine how the respective artists' parodic repetitions of settler landscapes expose and destabilize their meanings. Next, Day turns to the transformation of constructions of Japanese labor vis-à-vis internment. Chapter 3, which looks at Joy Kogawa's novel *Obasan* and Rea Tajiri's experimental film memoir *History and Memory,* will be of especial interest to *NAIS* readers due to its relational analysis of white, Indigenous, and Japanese diasporic subjectivity. Day's discussion of Kogawa and Tajiri's texts illuminates the cultural transformation of Japanese diasporas in North America, from foreign "yellow peril" (pre-internment) to Indigenized surplus labor (post-internment). Day suggests that this transformation was conditioned through identifications of Japanese populations with Jews prior to internment, and identifications with Indigenous peoples following expulsion and relocation. In chapter 4, Day turns to work by multimedia artist Ken Lum and Karen Tei Yamashita's novel *Tropic of Orange* in order to discern how late capitalism continues settler imperatives to exploit Asian labor, while fetishizing Asian bodies as the embodiment of capital. The book concludes with an epilogue reflecting on Tommy Ting's sculpture, *Machine,* and its challenges to capitalism's mystification of the relationship between labor and value.

Alien Capital offers readers a compelling look at how racialization, capitalism and settler-colonialism are intertwined. Given the triangulated model of settler—Indigenous—alien through which it investigates these linkages, however, I do wish that the book had situated itself in relation to the germinal work of scholars such as Sunera Thobani and Sherene Razack. For example, Thobani's *Exalted Subjects: Studies in the Making of Race and Nation in Canada* (2007) and Razack's 2002 edited collection *Race, Space and the Law: Unmapping a White Settler Society* both define white settler societies through a triangulated framework that parallels Day's formulation. The inclusion of such a conversation would have helped to emphasize the significance of *Alien Capital* in relation to ongoing discussion of race, racialization, and settler-colonialism, and in particular the relational distinctions between U.S. and Canadian forms of settler-colonialism. This does not detract, however, from the impressive, layered analytical work that Day carries out in her book. I highly recommend *Alien Capital* for Native American and Indigenous studies scholars with an interest in settler-colonialism, critical ethnic studies, women's, gender, and sexuality studies, visual cultures, and literature.

BEENASH JAFRI is visiting assistant professor of American studies and gender, sexuality, and women's studies at University of California Davis and assistant professor in crime and justice studies at the University of Massachusetts Dartmouth.

JACKI THOMPSON RAND

The Beginning and End of Rape: Confronting Sexual Violence
in Native America
by Sarah Deer
University of Minnesota Press, 2015

LAWYER, SCHOLAR, and 2014 MacArthur fellow Sarah Deer (Muscogee Creek Nation) has a critically rigorous vision for confronting sexual violence in Native America. Her vision, located in an intersection formed by history, U.S. criminal law, tribal governance, and women's stories of sexual violence, offers a response to a five-hundred-year-old human rights travesty. Violence against Native women, long ignored as Deer explains, pierced the political and public consciousness upon the release of findings claiming that one in three Native American women experience sexual violence in the United States. A decade and a half has passed since the stark and startling figure entered, gendered, and changed the discourse on the state of Native America. But we are no closer to the solution, in part because of an academic preoccupation with numbers and an unattainable degree of statistical certainty given the population size, leading Deer to pose the damning question: how much more do we need to know in order to address the catastrophic level of violence against Native women? She has not been idle. The vision revealed in *The Beginning and End of Rape* is the outcome of Deer's decades-long community-based work with Native women, scholarship, legislative work, consultations with tribal governments, and dedicated search for Native women's voices in the archive of a dark, violent colonial history.

The subject matter itself is intimidating in its complexity for the average reader, which Deer seeks to explicate for a broad audience. Historically, white men have raped women with impunity, a fact so repulsive and shameful that it has to be explained in colonial logic of war spoils and aberrant frontier behaviors. Deer explains the persistence of interracial sexual violence against Native as an outcome of U.S. attacks on tribal sovereignty, particularly regarding tribal legal systems in the late nineteenth century. The 1885 Major Crimes Act, which covers rape, extended federal jurisdiction over American Indian tribes, stripping them of power to address such crimes. The 1978 *Oliphant* decision further tied the hands of tribal governments by divesting tribal courts of criminal jurisdiction over non-Indians. Simultaneously, federal prosecutors, working within a Western framework in which rape cases have until the late twentieth century been treated as an offshoot of property law, have systematically failed to prosecute such crimes. Native women have entered the twenty-first century unable to expect justice or accountability from the United States legal system. The result is that Native women, both reservation and urban, live with the high likelihood that they will experience rape in their lifetime. Although Deer has been engaged in work that has brought two important federal reforms, the Violence Against Women Act and the Tribal Law and Order Act, she argues that the most effective intervention in violence against Native women must come from the tribes.

Deer wishes to see tribal governments take on sexual violence in their communities in an all-encompassing, tribally specific way, predicated on the idea of a theory of Indigenous jurisprudence, the capstone of her work. For Deer, it is not enough to reverse history and fully restore tribal self-determinative government. She calls on tribes to forcefully articulate an antirape sentiment in policy, formulate rape codes and remedies that are historically and culturally informed, and attend to their own stories about how their ancestors responded to violence and restored peace. The aim of this theory is to address the crime, but also to reverse the destruction that spins out among kin and community when a women is sexually violated. In doing so, the system acknowledges the victim's self-determination rights and, simultaneously, the ways they are intertwined with that of the tribal government. Interracial sexual violence against Native women, for Deer and others, is a political act that strikes at the heart of tribal sovereignty, which her book compellingly illuminates. An Indigenous jurisprudence, embodied in carefully constructed definitions of violence, criminal codes, and codified consequences, reaffirms that sovereignty through the resolution of conflict and violence, return of peace, and restoration of a victim's dignity.

For the inexpert reader, there is much to take in on the issue of violence against Native women. Deer aims to provide the reader with clear explanations of many moving parts, including historical and legal precedents, violence by the largely unsatisfactory numbers, and the impact on victims and communities. While not seamless, and sometimes a bit ahistorical, the work is significant for what it reveals about the evolution of Deer's thought, shaped by many years of working in this complex terrain, particularly as it pertains to potential solutions to this catastrophic chapter in American Indian history.

JACKI THOMPSON RAND (Choctaw Nation of Oklahoma) is associate professor in the Department of History at the University of Iowa.

JEAN DENNISON

Those Who Belong: Identity, Family, Blood, and Citizenship
   among the White Earth Anishinaabeg
by Jill Doerfler
Michigan State University Press, 2015

IN THIS POINTED INVESTIGATION into citizenship debates among the Anishinaabeg of the White Earth Nation and the Minnesota Chippewa Tribe, Jill Doerfler provides a powerful model for decolonizing scholarship today. Working with her own community, she not only demonstrates how scholarship can be directly put to the service of complex Native nation debates, but also shows how we can theorize from and with Indigenous peoples, academics, histories, and stories. Unburdened by traditional disciplinary boundaries, Doerfler weaves together participatory ethnography, archival history, and literary criticism, demonstrating the true potential of American Indian studies today.

Those Who Belong begins with an excerpt from a 1913 federal investigation that attempted to map the blood quantum percentages of two hundred White Earth families. When asked about another man's status as either mixed or full blood, Ay-dow-ah-cumig-o-quay responded, "He is dead long ago. I don't know exactly what he was. You can go dig him out of his grave, and then you can find out" (xxi). From this provocative quip, Doerfler demonstrates the lack of resonance blood quantum had for Anishinaabeg in the early twentieth century, how this concept was imposed through problematic Euro-American scientific practice and governmental policy, and ultimately how blood quantum works against Native survivance.

Pulling heavily on Anishinaabe scholar Gerald Vizenor to theorize her primary terms, Doerfler argues throughout the text for Indigenous survivance—that is, a "reimagination of sovereignty that brings control to tribal nations and encompasses political status, resistance, cultural values, and traditions" (xxxii). While making an important contribution to Indigenous theories of sovereignty, this work also challenges the partition of theory and evidence. Using Vizenor's writing simultaneously as a primary text to understand the stakes of belonging among the Anishinaabeg and as an analytical tool to demonstrate the relevance of these discussions for a larger audience, Doerfler breaks down some of the colonizing binaries commonly found in scholarship.

From archival documents, Doerfler tells the story of continued Anishinaabeg resistance to various federal government attempts at consolidation and erasure, particularly during the 1910s and 1930s. Through this evidence she demonstrates how it was family, not blood quantum, that was the central organizing principle for the Anishinaabeg and how they repeatedly refused the imposition of federal government narratives. Tying citizenship numbers to the strength of a Native nation, Doerfler clearly demonstrates how blood quantum was a tool for elimination and thus colonization.

In chapter 3, Doerfler turns to the citizenship debates surrounding the twenty-first-century White Earth Nation constitutional convention. This chapter is a powerful example of how scholarship can work within and be part of emergent moments of community change. Describing the constitutional process and her role in detail, this chapter serves as a history for the community, a guide for other nations seeking governmental reform, as well as a grounded interrogation of blood quantum as a tool for citizenship. Rather than seeking to understand the motivations behind each perspective, the chapter, like the text as a whole, demonstrates the importance of scholarly advocacy in the face of ongoing colonialism. As the canonical scholar Linda Smith argues, "Research is not an innocent or distant academic exercise but an activity that has something at stake and that occurs in a set of political and social conditions" (*Decolonizing Methodology: Research and Indigenous Peoples* [London: Zed Books, 1999], 5). Throughout the text, Doerfler argues adamantly for overturning blood quantum standards and the colonial legacies they contain.

In concluding *Those Who Belong* with an Anishinaabe story, Doerfler demonstrates the true potential of theorizing from Indigenous values and traditions. Indigenous stories are too often selectively used to reinforce static notions of Indigenous peoples as a uniform primitive people with values fundamentally at odds with the modern world. Doerfler instead tells the Earthdiver story, which is about fundamental change in the face of massive destruction. This story of rebirth powerfully speaks to the potential of Indigenous people not just to survive in the current moment, but to thrive through transformation and constant motion, or what, again drawing on Vizenor, she terms transmotion: "If they had not taken action, Nanaboozhoo and the animals would have been the victims of the flood. Instead, they worked together to create a new place for themselves—they engaged in transmotion and rebuilt" (93). Crossing not only disciplinary boundaries but also the omnipresent separation between theory and action, Doerfler theorizes from core Anishinaabe values of family connection and survivance, demonstrating the decolonizing potential of American Indian scholarship today.

JEAN DENNISON (Osage Nation) is assistant professor of anthropology at the University of Washington.

ROSE STREMLAU

Asegi Stories: Cherokee Queer and Two-Spirit Memory
by Qwo-Li Driskill
University of Arizona Press, 2016

IN *ASEGI STORIES: CHEROKEE QUEER AND TWO-SPIRIT MEMORY*, Qwo-Li Driskill, a scholar of women, gender, and sexuality studies at Oregon State University, challenges historical interpretations that exclude Cherokees who did not / do not conform to binary gender roles or heterosexuality. Like the gap between the walls of a double woven basket, Driskill creates space between the colonial and postcolonial in which queer interpretations give insight about the past and fuel healing in the present. S/he does so in an introduction, five chapters, and epilogue. Driskill engages contradictory perspectives, which explains the use of *asegi. Asegi udanto* "refers, specifically, to people who either fall outside of men's and women's roles or who mix men's and women's roles." It literally translates as "strange" (5–6).

In the first chapter, Driskill invites queer theorists to pay attention to Indigeneity because Two-Spirit critiques of racism, misogyny, and homophobia challenge nationalist structures and make clear the role of sexism, homophobia, and transphobia in colonization. Two-Spirit activists also serve as models who have facilitated healing through the arts, the erotic, and the integration of the politics of the spirit and the land.

In chapter 2, Driskill provides an *asegi* reinterpretation of the Spanish invasion of Cofitachequi to demonstrate how heteropatriarchy informed colonization and our memory of it. Driskill argues that when creating records, colonists perceived *all* Cherokee people to be deviants and overlooked those engaged in same-gender relationships. S/he demonstrates how we, rather than assuming a static binary, can gain insight into Indigenous understandings when we look for "balance in a multidimensional, spherical cosmology constantly in motion and constantly at risk of imbalance" (47). The leader of Cofitachequi, described as feminine and subservient in most tellings, thus becomes *asegi* when re-storied as actively refusing to conform to the gendered expectations of the Spanish and engaging in a sexual relationship that defied their norms. Driskill then emphasizes how colonists conceptualized Indigenous women's bodies and land as available, an argument that has been a central concept in American Indian women's history since the release of Rayna Green's classic article on the "Pocahontas Perplex" in 1975. This literature is notably absent from the bibliography.

In the third chapter, Driskill analyzes two forces that undermined the traditional, dynamic balance that sustained gender and sexual diversity: chattel slavery and Christianity. This chapter would have been enriched by attention to the economic and social functions of slavery in the Native South as articulated by Alan Gallay and Christina Snyder. Likewise, discussions of the adaptation and internalization of the concept of race relied selectively on some of the work of Tiya Miles and Theda Perdue but ignored their other scholarship and that of Claudio Saunt and Fay A. Yarbrough. The author's critique would have been more effective had this rich literature been addressed in full.

In chapter 4, Driskill challenges modern-day Cherokee politicians who characterize traditional Cherokee sexuality as heterosexual and patriarchal. S/he reinterprets a ceremony described in the Payne-Butrick Papers and suggests that rather than "formalizing friendship" between men, this ritual acknowledged the existence of same-sex relationships and created a space for them within the clan system. S/he also analyzes erotic art that documents the existence of an irreverent, playful view of sexuality. Driskill asserts that before adopting Euro-American values, Cherokee "communities acknowledged numerous kinds of relationships and that there was nothing unusual about people of the same gender building one fire, heart, and hearth together" (147).

In the final chapter, Driskill interweaves interviews with four Cherokee people s/he identifies as *asegi*. Although s/he emphasized the importance of understanding *asegi* people in relationship with their communities in the first chapter, this section does not provide contextual information such as citizenship status (Cherokee Nation, United Keetoowah Band, or Eastern Band of Cherokee Indians), rural or urban, et cetera, that would have enabled readers' to have a greater appreciation of how these individuals understand themselves as part of their nation(s).

This is not a book that describes in detail the nonbinary gender constructions and nonheterosexual sexualities among Cherokees in the model of Walter L. Williams or Will Roscoe, and that is okay. Like Mark Rifkin in his *When Did Indians Become Straight? Kinship, the History of Sexuality, and Native Sovereignty*, Driskill calls for a reconceptualization of what we think we know about Cherokee gender and sexual norms and argues that awareness is an important component of the decolonizing process. There are good ideas in here, and I hope the author's future work picks up on the strands left unwoven in this book.

ROSE STREMLAU is professor in the History Department at Davidson College.

JOHN R. GRAM

The Railroad and the Pueblo Indians: The Impact of the Atchison, Topeka,
   and Santa Fe on the Pueblos of the Rio Grande, 1880–1930
by Richard H. Frost
University of Utah Press, 2016

WHILE BOTH RAILROADS AND NATIVE AMERICANS are plentiful in Western historiography, Frost argues that the two are seldom considered together—at least not in a fruitful way. According to Frost, historians of the railroads often write "with nothing more than nineteenth-century ideas about Indians" (1), while Indian historians fail to consider the effects that railroads had on the communities they are studying. Frost's book, then, can be understood as an attempt to marry railroad history with the new Indian history by examining the relationship between the AT&SF railroad mentioned in the title and the Pueblo communities in northern New Mexico.

To demonstrate the significant impact the railroads had on the Pueblos, Frost focuses in particular on the communities of Laguna and Santo Domingo. These two communities represent very different responses along the continuum of Pueblo–railroad relations. Frost argues that Laguna, a more "progressive" community, benefited from the railroads in important ways, while Santo Domingo, a more "traditional" community, probably suffered the most. Furthermore, while interactions with the railroads did not turn Laguna "progressive" or Santo Domingo "traditional," Frost argues that their response to the railroads confirmed—even exacerbated—both communities' trajectories heading into the twentieth century. This part of the book is particularly strong, and effectively demonstrates the utility of Frost's project in bringing railroad and Indian history together.

Frost's convincingly demonstrates the significant impact the AT&SF had on Pueblo communities. The railroad stole significant amounts of land on which to lay tracks and to build supporting structures. The location of tracks could disrupt Pueblo irrigation, and even threaten Pueblo water rights themselves. AT&SF attempts to grab land also brought to the spotlight the fragility of some pueblos' claims to their own land in the new U.S. territory, opening up a path for the territorial government and Anglo settlers to challenge these claims as well. The new presence of trains near these communities meant injuries and loss of life for both the Pueblos and their livestock. In fact, the original tracks for the AT&SF actually ran right through the middle of Laguna pueblo before being moved later. Frost also focuses on the piecemeal and often haphazard decision making that led to the presence of the AT&SF in northern New Mexico in the first place. In discussing the railroad's motives for and methods of spreading across the Southwest, Frost effectively challenges both the romanticism sometimes still associated with Western expansion of railroads (Frost argues that the AT&SF enjoys a particularly rosy popular perception), as well as that peculiar sense of "destiny" that still colors American expansion itself.

Frost rightly recognizes that the relationship between the Pueblos and the AT&SF did not occur in a vacuum. He does an excellent job of showing how various other forces, such as federal boarding schools, the territorial government, and Anglo settlers, made a significant impact on the Pueblos at the turn of the century. His discussion of these things would serve as a helpful introduction for anyone working in the field. He also manages to tie the relationship between the Pueblos and these other actors back to the influence of the railroads. That said, the importance of the railroads is sometimes lost. At times it is clear why the railroad matters to the relationship between the Pueblos and the federal schools, as one example. At other times, however, the connection seems more tangential. The AT&SF sometimes fails to pull its weight in this sort of dual biography, as these other factors steal its spotlight for portions of the book.

Although determining if the Pueblos were ultimately better or worse off because of the invasion of the AT&SF railroad is not a main thrust of the book, Frost does consider it a question "worth asking" (6). Certainly Frost does not downplay the destructive influence of the AT&SF, but he does engage in value judgments about the legacy of American "modernity" for the Pueblos with which all readers may not agree. That said, Frost convincingly demonstrates the significant impact the AT&SF had on the northern New Mexico Pueblo communities—not only directly, but also through their influence on other actors. He also shows how valuable the new Indian history toolkit can be when examining the history of the Western railroads. Historians of both the Western railroads and of Western Indigenous communities would do well to incorporate his findings.

JOHN R. GRAM is an instructor in the History Department at Missouri State University.

BOYD COTHRAN

Surviving Wounded Knee: The Lakotas and the Politics of Memory
by David W. Grua
Oxford University Press, 2016

WOUNDED KNEE LOOMS LARGE in American history. It's remembered as a tragedy, a turning point, an ending. On December 29, 1890, along the banks of Wounded Knee Creek in South Dakota, the Seventh Cavalry—in revenge for the death of Lt. Colonel George Armstrong Custer, many would later say—killed more than two hundred Lakota Ghost Dancers, the last remnants of Indigenous resistance to American Manifest Destiny. The Indian wars were over. Civilization triumphed over savagery. And out of the Indian's last gasp, modernity emerged. Or so the story goes.

But as David Grua painstakingly documents in *Surviving Wounded Knee: The Lakotas and the Politics of Memory,* historical remembrances of the event have been hotly contested from the beginning. For the U.S. Army, the "battle"—as they insisted on calling it—was justified and heroic. Reporters and Colonel James W. Forsyth, the commander in charge, blamed the event on "fanatical" Ghost Dancers. In articles, official reports, and even throughout an initial investigation spearheaded by a skeptical Major General Nelson A. Miles, U.S. Army soldiers closed rank to exonerate Forsyth and the Seventh Cavalry. Portraying the Indian wars as a "race war" and the Lakota as "hostile" and "'treacherous savages,' who had killed their own women and children," the official record cast Wounded Knee as "the final victory in the four-hundred-year struggle between civilization and savagery for the continent" (80).

The official record, however, did not go unchallenged. As Grua shows, Lakota survivors pursued historical justice, following Lakota cultural practices of conflict resolution, by seeking compensation from the government. In 1896 they filed claims for compensation from the government for property loss during what they called, in opposition to the official record, "a massacre." They also constructed counter-memorials. In one of the most interesting sections of the book, Joseph Horn Cloud—who as a teenager lost his parents at Wounded Knee—and other survivors erected an obelisk "In Memory of the Chief Big Foot Massacre." Placing their monument at the Wounded Knee mass grave in 1903, the memorial included a list of those murdered by the Seventh Calvary with the Lakota inscription *"Cankpi Opi Eltona Wicakte Picun He Cajepi Kin—*'These are the Names of those Killed at Wounded Knee'" (101). The government ignored the claims, and the memorial.

But in 1904, Horn Cloud and others renewed their pursuit of justice by filing again for compensation. This time, the government investigated. And what followed were several decades of hearings and investigations by the Indian Office and even Congress. These hearings, and the historical documentations they produced, slowly shifted the language around the event from "battle" to "massacre," until finally South Dakota Congressman Francis Case introduced a bill in the 1930s intended to "liquidate the liability" of the United States for Wounded Knee by offering the survivors and their descendants some form of compensation. Although the bill ultimately failed and was abandoned in the wake of World War II, it was nonetheless, according to Grua, a "historical achievement" that represented a foundation for future political activism in the name of the tragedy of Wounded Knee (174).

Grua's work comes amid a decadelong explosion of scholarship on the historical legacies of nineteenth-century U.S.—Indian violence. And as such, it should be read in the context of similar studies such as the work of Lisa Blee, Chip Colwell-Chanthaphonh, Michael Elliott, Karl Jacoby, and Ari Kelman to name a few. Like these scholars, Grua exposes the layered ways in which political and economic power, memorial culture, and official and unofficial archives fundamentally structure our access to and understanding of the past, especially the violent past.

But unlike these other works, Grua's book only tangentially and very lightly engages with the politics of the past in the present. His study effectively ends in 1940. And although the publication of Dee Brown's *Bury My Heart at Wounded Knee* in 1970 and the American Indian Movement's occupation of Wounded Knee in 1973 are used to bookend his story, there is no effort to connect the politics of memory in the decades after Wounded Knee with the politics of memory in the twenty-first century. Bridging that gap and connecting the violence of the past with the ongoing politics of memory in America today would have given the work greater relevance. That said, Grua has provided a careful analysis of the early twentieth-century politics of memory of the most iconic and paradigmatic massacre in American history. And in the process, he has contributed to our ongoing reevaluation of the history of Indians wars through historical memory.

BOYD COTHRAN is associate professor in the Department of History at York University.

CHELSEA D. FRAZIER

Métis and the Medicine Line: Creating a Border and Dividing a People
by Michael Hogue
Chapel Hill: University of North Carolina Press, 2015

BETWEEN 1872 AND 1874 the British North American Boundary Commission began to construct sod-covered earthen mounds to demarcate the United States from Canadian territory. The Plains Métis served as scouts to help guide the surveyors along the 49th parallel. Michel Hogue states in his introduction that this process made "an invisible border . . . visible" (1). Hogue argues that the Plains Métis played a crucial role in shaping the borderlands region around the 49th parallel. He concludes that the Métis shaped state-building and race-making on both the Canadian and U.S. side of the border.

The emergence of the Plains Métis with cultural interactions founded in the fur trade shaped the region as this practice displaced Indigenous peoples in the area. Hogue traces the emergence of the Plains Métis to the large network of French trading posts in the Great Lakes region during the eighteenth century. As fur trading extended westward so, too, did the Métis. This process, as Hogue argues, allowed for the solidification of distinct Métis populations and communities in the West (26). The Métis became political actors as their communities relied on the buffalo herds in the region that resided on both sides of the border.

By the 1860s, Hogue argues that Plains traders were part of a competitive transnational commercial network of buffalo, which solidified Métis settlements in the borderlands region (60). These fur trade communities evolved into more agrarian settlements, especially in the Red River Valley. Hogue demonstrates that the Western borderlands region was incorporated into the United States and Canada at different rates because of the arrival of railroads south of the border. As both countries gained more control over the region it caused both nations to exert their authority over Indigenous peoples differently. Hogue asserts that differences between the United States and Canada existed in the 1870s, because Canada held a more precarious role as it had only recently entered the region and the Métis were strong because of the foundations set by the Hudson's Bay Company. Hogue concludes that exchange allowed the Métis to adapt to the changes, despite the attempts by the United States and Canada to exert more control over the region.

After the emergence of the Métis, Hogue argues that they continued to face issues of sovereignty and race in the 1870s. The relations on the Northern Plains in this era grew more tenuous with the 1876 Great Sioux War and the 1877 Nez Perce War. Hogue agrees with other scholars in arguing that the shrinking buffalo population contributed to these conflicts (103). He ultimately determines that the borderlands of the 49th parallel attracted a larger population of Natives and Métis because of the continued existence of buffalo herds in the region.

Throughout the 1870s both the United States and Canada began to "assign ethnic and racial labels," which provided the impetus for the Métis to solidify their belonging by seeking state sanctions (140). By 1879, Hogue argues, the American and Canadian officials restricted movement across the border hoping to break down Métis networks (145). Both nations did not like the growing number of Indigenous people on the border as they feared it undermined federal Indian politics (153). Despite the growing control of the Canadian and American officials the Métis continued to cross the border.

Hogue argues that as the Métis continued to cross the border both governments began to examine both legal and political consequences of the border crossing (184). As the governments came to terms with the continued border crossing, Hogue demonstrates that they reevaluated earlier borderland policies to fit more readily with concepts of both nation and race. By demonstrating these shifting ideas surrounding social relations Hogue clearly shows how the Métis shaped the formation of the borderlands surrounding the 49th parallel.

With *Métis and the Medicine Line,* Michel Hogue has successfully established that the relationships formed along the 49th parallel shaped both the politics and race relations of the region. Additionally, he demonstrates that both the U.S. Indian policy and Canadian policies shaped the way those nations treated the Métis populations. Hogue sets up his argument clearly in the beginning; however, this is not seen throughout the work as his argument gets lost in the details. Despite this minor flaw Hogue expands our understanding of the complex relationship that existed on the Northern Great Plains in the nineteenth century.

CHELSEA D. FRAZIER is a doctoral student in the Department of History at the University of Oklahoma.

KEVIN BRUYNEEL

Redskins: Insult and Brand
by C. Richard King
University of Nebraska, 2016

IN MAY 2016, the *Washington Post* published the results of a poll in which 90 percent of "Native Americans" surveyed were not offended by "Redskins," the
name of the Washington, D.C., professional football team. Self-identification
as a Native person—not as a confirmed citizen of a particular Indigenous nation—was all the *Post* required of respondents to validate identity. Defenders of the name, the vast majority of whom are white people (including the
team owner, Dan Snyder), welcomed these results as confirming their view
that the name was of concern only to politically correct white liberals, not
Indigenous people. The poll and response to it reflects a deeper dynamic in
the history of the Washington team name, for as C. Richard King states in
his excellent book *Redskins: Insult and Brand,* "Too often, Native American
opinion matters only because of how whites use it. It cannot be heard in its
original voice, terms, or context" (142). As with the team name, the *Post* poll
is a form of white appropriation and construction of Indigeneity produced for
the consumption of, primarily, white Americans, with little to no regard for
Indigenous people's "voice, terms, or context." This is U.S. settler-colonialism
in practice, in which Americans "absorb indigeneity, laying claim to indigenous people's rightful inheritance while lamenting nostalgically their passing" (24). To underscore the deeper imperative here, King builds on Patrick
Wolfe's concept of "the logic of elimination," according to which "indigenous
people must be disappeared" for Americans to establish and justify their
claim to and sense of belonging on dispossessed Indigenous territory (51).

The appropriation of Indigenous land, absorption of identity, and efforts
to make Indigenous people disappear are intertwined elements of settler-
colonialism. This is why the political struggle over the Washington football
team matters, and why King's book is a must-read for anyone interested in
this issue and how settler-colonialism functions in relationship to it. After
the introduction, King covers much of what one must know about this topic.
He begins with the "Origins" and "Uses" (chapters 2 and 3) of the name, then
turns to the "Erasure" of Indigenous voices (chapter 4), the "Sentiment" settlers invest in the name (chapter 5), the importance of the "Black/White" racial dynamic (chapter 6), the role of "Ownership" in many forms (chapter 7),
the "Simulation" of Indigenous support for the name, and the problematic
function of "Opinion" (chapters 8 and 9). King closes by considering what

"Change" might look like in this case and the "Ends" that could be served by such change (chapters 10 and 11).

The book's most impressive element is the well-sourced historical narrative and the emphasis on detailing the multiple actors and institutions implicated in the Washington team name and the political struggle over it, with a strong account of the different forms of Indigenous resistance going back decades. As well, King provides worthy theoretical insights, as exemplified in the "Sentiment" chapter in which he argues that the "affective attachment" people have in the team name as a "mnemonic device" dissociates fans from their relationship to racism and colonialism in our time (66–67), and in the chapter on "Ownership" where he persuasively asserts the importance of understanding how "empire and exploitation, capital and conquest form the unspoken and unexamined foundations of racialized entitlement" (96). King thus deftly accounts for the fact that the psychic-libidinal and political economies of racism and settler-colonialism are simultaneously at work in the Washington team name case. At times, King does turn to more liberal, rather than radical, political approaches for addressing this issue, such as recommending greater "critical literacy" education to counter the incapacity of white Americans to think about or remember the history of erasure, violence, and appropriation against Indigenous people (54–57). These recommendations run into slight conflict with the fact that King's study shows that education and remembering can only go so far, as the power of white settler disavowal—to have knowledge but not acknowledge its political implications—often overwhelms the best efforts of educators. More knowledge does not necessarily liberate, but it can provide important resources for political efforts and argument. In this regard, King's book offers a basis for an anticolonial politics that confronts white settler psychic and economic investments in disappearing and dispossessed Indigeneity, as reflected and reproduced in the Washington team name. For this and many other reasons, *Redskins: Insult and Brand* is a vital work that will make a significant impact on our grasp of and debate over this issue.

KEVIN BRUYNEEL is professor of politics in the History and Society Division of Babson College in Wellesley, Massachusetts.

CURTIS FOXLEY

An American Genocide: The United States and the California Indian
*   Catastrophe, 1846–1873*
by Benjamin Madley
Yale University Press, 2016

GENOCIDE IS A MODERN WORD that describes a process deeply rooted in history. First coined in 1943 by the legal scholar Raphael Lemkin, "genocide" combines the Greek word *genos* (tribe or race) and the Latin *cide* (killing), to encapsulate "any attempt to physically or culturally annihilate an ethnic, national, religious, or political group" (4). Five years after Lemkin put the word "genocide" to paper, the United Nations Convention on the Prevention and Punishment of the Crime of Genocide constructed a narrower definition of the term. Although the United Nations cannot retroactively prosecute genocidal crimes that occurred before 1948, the historian Benjamin Madley maintains that its definition of genocide provides "a powerful analytical tool: a frame for evaluating the past and comparing similar events across time" (5). Beginning in 1968, scholars began using the term to describe the nineteenth-century U.S. conquest of California. More recently, some historians, such as Gary Clayton Anderson, have questioned whether the collapse of California's Native American population was an act of genocide or, alternatively, a process of ethnic cleansing. In *An American Genocide,* Madley not only proves that genocide did, indeed, occur in nineteenth-century California, he also carefully explains how the process developed over time.

Although Madley recognizes that disease, starvation, and exposure helped decimate California's Native American population between 1846 and 1873, his documentation of Anglo-American violence toward Native Americans demonstrates that shootings, stabbings, hangings, and beheadings significantly contributed to the destruction of California Native Americans. Taking a comprehensive, year-by-year approach, Madley fills each chapter of *An American Genocide* with genocidal acts. These atrocities include the Sacramento River Massacre, the Bloody Island Massacre, and other genocidal killings that contemporaries falsely publicized as "wars." Anglo-Americans committed these genocidal acts against Native Americans, such as the Hupa, Yuki, and Modoc, for a variety of reasons. In some instances, genocidal violence was a harsh response to smaller offenses, such as isolated murders and theft. In other cases, Anglo-Americans practiced what Madley calls "pedagogic killing" (217). That is to say, some Anglos murdered Native Americans to demonstrate their power and place in Californian society. Still other Anglos attempted to exterminate Native Americans to seize their land and remove them from their competitors' labor supply.

Even though Madley is not the first historian to describe the destruction of California Native Americans as genocide, his work is nonetheless distinctive. *An American Genocide* moves the historiography forward by identifying how genocide in California unfolded and developed as a process, or a trajectory. When Anglo-Americans arrived in California, they initially attempted to maintain the social hierarchy and system that the Spaniards and Mexicans created in California. This consisted of enslaving and dehumanizing Native Americans. Shortly before the gold rush, this system gave way to vigilante killings. Later, state legislators passed laws that kept Native Americans excluded from the political process and left them vulnerable to Anglo violence. Finally, the federal government perfected "the killing machine" when it reimbursed the State of California nearly $1 million for the costs associated with killing Native Americans (230). By the time of the Civil War, genocide was "primarily a federal project" fueled by federal dollars and manned by the U.S. Army (300).

While violence does appear to have escalated over time, Madley struggles to demonstrate how Anglo-American rule differed from the Mexican experience. For example, Madley explains that Anglo-Americans "sought to *maintain*" the Spanish and Mexican social and economic systems that dehumanized, enslaved, abused, and killed California Native Americans (145, emphasis mine). However, Madley later insists that Anglo-Americans "*began* a protracted process" when they "stripped California Indians of legal power and rights, excluded them from colonial society, deprived them of their land, denied them protection, legalized their exploitation as both de jure and de factor unfree laborers, and ultimately all but erased legal and cultural barriers to their abuse and murder" (146, emphasis mine). In short, Madley does not decide, or clearly convey, whether Anglo-Americans maintained the Spanish and Mexican model, modified it, or began a new process.

Despite this flaw, *An American Genocide* is an important text. Readers interested in Californian history, the gold rush, or Native American history will find this text horrifying but useful. Perhaps the most impressive aspect of *An American Genocide* is its appendices. Readers will be stunned and saddened when they read the 191 pages of tables that document killings, massacres, state militia campaigns, and U.S. Army operations against California Native Americans. This inventory of violence should be enough to convince skeptics that genocide did, indeed, occur in California.

CURTIS FOXLEY is a PhD student in the Department of History at the University of Oklahoma.

CATHERINE J. DENIAL

Illicit Love: Interracial Sex and Marriage in the United States and Australia
by Ann McGrath
University of Nebraska Press, 2016

WHEN HISTORIANS TACKLE THE TRANSNATIONAL, they most often do so across nation-state borders, comparing India with Pakistan, or France with Germany, for example. Ann McGrath expands our sense of the transnational to look at the workings of nations contained within one country—here, the Cherokee and the United States, and Aboriginal people and Australia. McGrath's goal is not to create a direct comparison, as much divides these two locales: geography, place-making, time period, and culture, to name just a few. Instead, McGrath seeks to examine both colonization and resistance through the lens of marriage, and argues that it is in the micro, intimate history of a place that we can best see the fractures in colonialist policy.

The micro-histories that make up the first four chapters of the book are particularly strong. McGrath takes single relationships—Harriet Gold and Elias Boudinot in 1820s America, John Ross and Mary Bryan Stapler in the United States of the 1840s, Ernest Gribble and Jeannie in Australia at the turn of twentieth century—and demonstrates that the personal is unavoidably political when one is marrying not only across color lines but across national borders. McGrath anchors us in the most private correspondence—courtship letters and confessional prose written to close friends—unpacking these sources to demonstrate the larger fortunes of the colonial enterprise. We become party to the places where Cherokee and Aboriginal people undermined the colonial experiment by holding fast to their own ideas about marriage, gender, land, and power. We see the places where settler colonists worked violent change on landscapes, peoples, and ideas with the force of their racial beliefs—by removing both the Cherokee and Indigenous Australians from their ancestral homes, for example. We become familiar with the ways in which resistance could manifest in the choice of a sexual or romantic partner, in the decision to have a child, or in the place a person lived—it was not simply enacted through the business of treaties and war. Marriage exists at the heart of a tangled web of personal choices and national policy, argues McGrath, making it the perfect vehicle to explore nation-making and unmaking in settler-colonist states.

McGrath's focus enlarges in the third and fourth sections of her book to analyze policies that had an effect on wide swathes of people, while still being anchored in the idea of marriage. She examines the Australian government's policy of inquiring into an Aboriginal woman's consent to marry a non-Aboriginal partner, the practice of polygamy in the United States and Australia, and the Cherokee nation's policies regarding intermarriage between non-Native men and Cherokee women (and vice versa). In each instance, she demonstrates the limits of the settler-colonial state to create the "pure" nation that so many white supremacist thinkers wanted, as well as the limitations of national sovereignty among Cherokee and Aboriginal peoples' to police the physical and affectionate boundaries of their cultures. With marriage as our focus, we see the untidiness of the settler-colonist venture, the practice of nation-making and maintenance, and the weak spots in imperial and national designs.

That the case studies at the heart of this volume are not directly comparable does make for some cognitive hiccups—one cannot help but search for comparisons where none are meant. But in thinking about marriage as a researcher's tool, a magnifying glass that causes cracks and fissures to pop into focus, the book has much to recommend it as a think piece in exploring how marriage might transform what we think we know about sovereignty, imperial incursions, and Indigenous resistance to the same.

CATHERINE J. DENIAL is Bright Professor of American History and chair of the History Department at Knox College.

DAVID UAHIKEAIKALEI'OHU MAILE

Kanaka 'Ōiwi Methodologies: Mo'olelo and Metaphor
edited by Katrina-Ann R. Kapā'anaokalāokeola Nākoa Oliveira
   and Erin Kahunawaika'ala Wright
University of Hawai'i Press, 2016

IN THIS FOURTH VOLUME of the Hawai'inuiākea School of Hawaiian Knowledge's series, the editors trace and argue for methodologies, and methods, to scholarship that are unapologetically Kanaka 'Ōiwi. In doing so, Katrina-Ann R. Kapā'anaokalāokeola Nākoa Oliveira and Erin Kahunawaika'ala Wright suggest the anthology has two aims. The first is to foster dialogue across various Kanaka 'Ōiwi methodological approaches to producing knowledge. The second is to advance the diverse ways that Kānaka 'Ōiwi engage, practice, and apply scholarly research. Different from previous volumes in the Hawai'inuiākea series, *Kanaka 'Ōiwi Methodologies* untangles the complexly interwoven frameworks that animate and equip 'Ōiwi researchers in the study of 'ike Hawai'i, or Hawaiian knowledge.

The authors offer readers mo'olelo (stories, narratives, histories) and metaphors as organizing concepts rooted in Indigenous Hawaiian epistemologies. Much of this work is positioned from the field of education. Kaiwipunikauikawēkiu Lipe suggests mo'olelo expressed in oli (chants) and 'ōlelo no'eau (proverbs) are imbued with metaphorical meanings for 'Ōiwi survival. In turn, she suggests "mo'olelo aku, mo'olelo mai" (54), or sharing and receiving mo'olelo. For Lipe, this is an engaged practice and methodology, especially to transform wahine (female) leadership in struggles against the racism and patriarchy of the academy. By highlighting King David Kalākaua's mele "Ua Noho Au A Kupa I Ke Alo," R. Keawe Lopes Jr. recommends a research protocol responsible and accountable to kūpuna (elders), community participants, practitioners, and teachers as mentors. Coalescing these arguments, Maya L. Kawailanaokeawaiki Saffery's essay, analyzing place-based educational programming, demonstrates how mele (songs) and hula (dances) communicate mo'olelo, like that of Queen Emma's journey to Mauna a Wākea in 1874, which metaphorically and materially ground 'Ōiwi scholars to geographic ways of being in the 'āina, or the land that feeds us, of Hawai'i.

Other authors outline 'Ōiwi methodologies from a more explicitly environmental and 'āina-based focus. Extending environmental studies, Mehana Blaich Vaughan reflects on research in Lumaha'i Valley on Kaua'i with the Waipā Foundation. Sharing three lessons from this project, Vaughan contends 'āina is a source as well as guiding partner, 'āina links communities, and 'āina emboldens our connections to place. In the essay written by Katrina-Ann R.

Kapāʻanaokalāokeola Nākoa Oliveira, wai (fresh water) presents a metaphor to map how scholarly contributions by Kānaka ʻŌiwi collectively constitute ʻike Hawaiʻi, like streams flowing into the ocean. For instance, Oliveira argues that academic inquiry written in ʻōlelo Hawaiʻi (Hawaiian language) and utilizing the vast archives of Hawaiian-language texts signifies ancestral wisdom as the source of these running waters. Thus, Summer Puanani Maunakea theorizes an aloha ʻāina framework based on and utilizing ʻike kupuna (ancestral knowledge). Brandy Nālani McDougall's story "Nā ʻIliʻili" illuminates the regenerative force of ʻike kūpuna through the metaphorical use of the moʻo (lizard). "ʻŌiwi scholars across a range of academic disciplines and institutions of higher education," according to Maunakea, "are thriving, driven by our kuleana to our ʻohana, our people, and our ʻāina" (142–43).

This volume powerfully shows that Hawaiian studies is a capacious, dynamic, and critical field. In her indispensible chapter, Noelani Goodyear-Kaʻōpua tracks a genealogy of ʻŌiwi methodologies. She situates Hawaiian studies as an interdisciplinary field with four commitments: lāhui (collective identity, self-definition), ea (sovereignty, leadership), kuleana (positionality, obligations), and pono (harmonious relationships, justice, healing). By invoking Haunani-Kay Trask's poem "Sons," Goodyear-Kaʻōpua asserts that these intersecting concepts metaphorically signify ʻaho (single cords) that, when plaited together, reproduce ropes of resistance against injustice, violence, and elimination. Erin Kahunawaikaʻala Wright and Brandi Jean Nālani Balutski's essay illustrates this interdisciplinary methodology and analytical intersectionality. Building on the work of critical race and tribal critical race theorists, they conceptualize an ʻŌiwi critical race theory in order to critique structural forms of oppression, such as U.S. hegemony, settler-colonialism, corporate tourism, and military occupation, that have systematically marginalized our lāhui.

Kanaka ʻŌiwi Methodologies sketches out how Kānaka ʻŌiwi, disciplined by various fields of study, center Indigenous Hawaiian epistemologies as analytical tools. This is a profound intervention, which contributes to Hawaiian studies but also Native American and Indigenous studies at large. Therefore, the anthology's impact is not simply articulated by casting Kānaka ʻŌiwi as subjects of knowledge production rather than objects to study, but by contending that the theoretical frameworks and methods of analysis shaping this knowledge, like moʻolelo and metaphor, are Kanaka ʻŌiwi. This work shouldn't be reductively abstracted as exotic or essentialist. Instead, it should be genuinely grappled with by Kānaka ʻŌiwi crafting ʻike Hawaiʻi, in undergraduate and graduate courses as well as *outside* the academy.

DAVID UAHIKEAIKALEIʻOHU MAILE (Kanaka Maoli) is a doctoral student in American studies at the University of New Mexico.

KAHENTE HORN-MILLER

Who Are These People Anyway?
by Chief Irving Powless, Jr., of the Onondaga Nation,
    edited by Lesley Forrester
Syracuse University Press, 2016

FORRESTER IN THIS SECOND COMPILATION attempts to re-create her original work *And Grandma Said . . . Iroquois Teaching as Passed Down through the Oral Tradition. Who Are These People Anyway?* presents itself as a collection of short stories, thoughts, and vignettes that are reflections of Onondaga elder Irving Powless. This work is meant to be framed around the question posed in the book's title: Who are these people anyway? As Powless indicated to Forrester, Indigenous peoples have been asking this about the newcomers since earliest contact.

This work, as Forrester describes, is an attempt to portray the living, spiritually—vitality of the Haudenosaunee. It is meant to turn the lens around and subject the newcomers to analysis. Tongue-in-cheek, scathing, a natural response Forrester writes, to the centuries of stereotyping and misunderstanding. She describes being asked to turn off the recorder and Powless then would continue with rich stories, which she expected would eventually become central to this work. As their relationship strengthened and Forrester gained the trust of Powless, the microphone was left on. As a result, the book is presented as a collection of reflections from a man who has lived for a long time in one place, the Onondaga Nation. One can imagine sitting in the room with elder Powless as he described his life. The richness of his stories is hinted at in this work but not fully articulated for our benefit.

Forrester's goal was to portray Haudenosaunee culture through Powless's eyes and to document it for future generations. Forrester only partially succeeds in this endeavor. The strength of this work lies in the glimpse we get of Powless's life in the twentieth century and his reflections on the meaning of the treaties and treaty process. The value in Powless's anecdotal reflections on the impacts of the treaty process, and their subsequent violation, serve in making these painful points in history meaningful and palatable for a wider audience. Yet Forrester is remiss in not contextualizing these important points in history, and as a result some value is lost to the reader. Additionally, when reading this work, one cannot help but ask who is the audience? And what value does this collection present for the various audiences that might read it?

Due to the disconnected nature of the chapter format that Forrester uses, the inherent fluidity of Indigenous storytelling is lost. Historical, social, and cultural contexts add richness, and without these contexts the "stories" in the short chapters feel as if they stand alone, each disconnected from the next. The reader is left hanging at the completion of each chapter. In her first work with elder Tom Porter, Forrester was successful in conveying both the fluidity and context of the Indigenous story. This new work does not draw you in with the same competency that her previous work does. Yet this work has its strengths, such as Powless's view on the treaty relationship, or the humor of his anecdotal reflections on the newcomers, lacrosse, and reservation life in the early twentieth century. Storytelling is about weaving together aspects of life, philosophy, and culture in a way that communicates important information that the listener learns. In this work the spoken words of elder Powless would have benefited from a more comprehensive approach by Forrester, one in which we are left feeling fulfilled by his important insights. Instead we are left with the expectancy that there is more to the stories. This book will likely be relevant to a general audience interested in knowing more about Haudenosaunee historical and contemporary life.

KAHENTE HORN-MILLER (Kanien:keha'ka) is assistant professor in the School of Indigenous and Canadian Studies at Carleton University in Ontario, Canada.

ALYSSA MT. PLEASANT

Seneca Art and Culture Center at Ganondagan State Historic Site
7100 County Road 41 (Boughton Hill Road), Victor, New York 14564
585-924-5848
http://www.ganondagan.org/

NESTLED IN ROLLING HILLS approximately twenty miles south of Rochester, New York, Ganondagan State Historic Site is the only New York State park devoted to Native American history and culture. Known as a seventeenth-century "town of peace" within the homelands of the Seneca Nation, Ganondagan has been a national historic landmark since the 1960s and was designated a state park in 1986. Since the 1980s G. Peter Jemison, Heron Clan of the Seneca Nation and longtime site manager, has developed an interpretive vision that includes a series of nature trails and a replica longhouse where public programming takes place. In October 2015 a new visitor center—the Seneca Art and Culture Center—opened at the historic site. This 17,300-square-foot facility is open year-round. It incorporates a permanent exhibit explaining the late seventeenth-century history of Ganondagan, a small screening room for the short film *Iroquois Creation Story* (2015), additional performance space and offices, as well as a gift shop.

While Ganondagan is a state park administered by the Department of Parks, Recreation, and Historic Preservation, the interpretive focus of the Seneca Art and Culture Center, as well as the larger 225-acre site, emphasizes Haudenosaunee (Iroquois) worldviews. The architecture of the Seneca Art and Culture Center, including the landscape design surrounding the new building and its adjacent parking area, incorporates elements of Haudenosaunee beliefs and practices. Approaching the center from the parking lot, visitors walk along the "thorny path," passing stone markers that gesture toward Haudenosaunee protocols for welcoming newcomers. These markers, along with a water feature and a small perpetual fire outside the entrance to the center, provide visitors with an initial orientation. Immediately inside the entryway, a large case of contemporary artwork and a video installation featuring a recitation of Ganonyo:k (the Words That Come Before All Else, or the Thanksgiving Address) further situate visitors within this Haudenosaunee place. Once inside the building, visitors may note that the floor plan of this modern structure features a central corridor illuminated by skylights, echoing the traditional architecture of Haudenosaunee longhouses where living quarters for numerous families were arranged on both sides of a central corridor; several fire pits positioned in the corridor, providing heat; and smoke holes in the roof, facilitating ventilation.

Haudenosaunee epistemologies are engaged more explicitly through the short film and exhibit that are central features of the Seneca Art and Culture Center. *Iroquois Creation Story,* a seventeen-minute film that was produced collaboratively by Ganondagan and Rochester Institute of Technology, combines animation with dance by traditional Haudenosaunee dancers and the Garth Fagan Dance Company. It tells the story of Skywoman, her descent from Skyworld, the formation of Turtle Island, and the origin of onkwehonwe (Indigenous peoples). Across from the screening room, the permanent exhibit develops a rich discussion of the Ganondagan settlement, situating the community within Haudenosaunee and colonial contexts. An initial panel titled "Onondowa'ga:' Ways of Knowing" alerts visitors to Seneca ways of understanding and transmitting knowledge that must be considered alongside European documentation practices and methodologies for interpreting the past. Throughout the permanent exhibit, panels and displays engage multiple approaches to the past, including oral traditions, the material record, and the documentary record. Additionally, while the exhibit emphasizes the seventeenth-century history of Ganondagan (including trade, diplomacy, violence, and daily life), modern Seneca life also features prominently. Panels highlighting music, dance, art, and language are complemented by videos and audio "storytelling stations" that bring contemporary Seneca voices into the exhibit. There is an entire wall dedicated to Iroquois Nationals lacrosse team.

The Seneca Art and Culture Center offers a detailed, nuanced interpretation of the seventeenth-century history of the community at Ganondagan. The permanent exhibit, featuring carefully selected objects and documents that are paired with thought-provoking panels, dioramas, video, and audio, offers numerous opportunities for engagement by visitors of all ages. One of the strengths of the exhibit is its integration of a wide range of primary sources (reproductions of archaeological artifacts as well as historic maps, documents, and artwork) that complement and reinforce narratives found in interpretive panels and labels. Docents also provide additional context about the exhibit and the larger historic site. For visitors unfamiliar with Haudenosaunee welcoming protocols, docents must explain the meaning and significance of markers leading to the center's entrance, as exterior signage does not currently provide this context. Similarly, the architectural references in the building can be revealed through conversation. Ganondagan offers robust programming during warmer weather and, although it is not immediately clear to visitors during the winter months, it is possible that decisions limiting signage and interpretation are intended to create sites for conversation on guided tours of the grounds.

ALYSSA MT. PLEASANT (Tuscarora) is assistant professor of Native American studies at the University at Buffalo (SUNY).

NADINE ATTEWELL

Hope at Sea: Possible Ecologies in Oceanic Literature
by Teresa Shewry
University of Minnesota Press, 2015

IN TERESA SHEWRY'S *HOPE AT SEA*, Pacific histories of environmental damage, loss, and possibility take center stage. Assembling a rich archive of poems, short stories, and novels, Shewry shows how literary texts contest (neo)colonial projects of resource extraction by imagining possibilities for different kinds of relationships with human and nonhuman others alike. In chapter 1, she reads *The Bone People* (1984), by the Māori writer Keri Hulme, in relation to Samuel Butler's 1872 novel *Erewhon,* focusing on the very different claims each makes on and about the future. Through readings of short fiction and poetry by two Asian diasporic writers from Hawaiʻi, Gary Pak and Cathy Song, chapter 2 attends to water's volatility and promise as a site of relation-making; while chapter 3 returns to Aotearoa New Zealand to think with poets Hone Tuwhare (Ngāpuhi), Cilla McQueen (Pākehā), and Ian Wedde (Pākehā) as they "struggle to regenerate the connections between human and nonhuman beings across long distances" (86). Water is also crucial to chapter 4's analysis of *Gould's Book of Fish,* a 2001 novel by the white Australian writer Richard Flanagan whose convict protagonist is bound to fish in a relationship that is at once terminally violent and complexly life-giving. Finally, in chapter 5, Shewry confronts histories of nuclear testing as they surface in Albert Wendt's dystopian classic *Black Rainbow* (1992) and Robert Barclay's *Melal* (2002). Each of the texts in Shewry's archive, then, grapples with "the existing world and its pasts" (166) even as they insist on the openness of the future. This, for Shewry, is what makes them hopeful: in the wake of loss, hope inheres in an attunement to the world as "characterized by both damage and potential" (175).

Given the heaviness of the histories with which we are (unevenly) burdened, Shewry's definition of hope is compelling. It also feels underdeveloped. Although Shewry notes that "hope" first drew her attention as a "term . . . in literary works that speak about environmental loss in a rapidly changing ocean" (178), she does not consistently track how the term operates in particular texts, leaving us to wonder whether hope resides "in" literary texts, or is generated in readers as they interact with texts. What kind of "thing" is hope? Is it an affect or an orientation? A geography, an aesthetics, or a relation? Why hope and not, say, futurity, or decolonization? The lack of precision in Shewry's conception of hope makes it difficult to know whether and how hope is something we could better cultivate, disseminate, or practice against the catastrophes that variously threaten us.

More puzzling is the book's limited engagement with the genealogies and frameworks of Pacific studies, Indigenous studies, postcolonial studies, and critical ethnic studies, this despite Shewry's insistence on the importance of working with "nonfiction theoretical writings, rather than only literature, from the Pacific" (17–18). The recent work of Alice Te Punga Somerville (*Once Were Pacific*) and Chadwick Allen (*Trans-Indigenous*) might have prompted Shewry to reflect further on the nature of the bonds that hold "the Pacific" together as a space, a collectivity, and an analytic. What underwrites the juxtaposition of, for example, Hawaiian cultural production with literature from Aotearoa New Zealand? How, furthermore, does it matter that the Hawai'i-based writers Shewry treats are of Asian descent, while the New Zealand–based writers identify either as (white) Pākehā or Māori? Such positional differences, which reflect divergent experiences of empire and capitalism, receive little attention in *Hope at Sea*. And yet, as scholars of the black and Asian diasporas have recently been concerned to show, diasporic people's relationships with the settler-colonial state and its pacifying projects are marked by their differential racialization. Attending to such differences, or to the particularity of Indigeneity as a geopolitical identity, would allow us to better understand both what is at stake in the practices of relation-making that interest Shewry, and why they are so difficult to sustain. Doing so would also highlight the politico-juridical mechanisms (such as land claims) through which Indigenous people have (strategically) worked to ensure their continued survival and that of the nonhuman beings with whom they are in relation, pursuing futures that may, but do not inevitably, align with diasporic interests. There is no doubt that, as Shewry argues, North American ecocriticism must be pushed "beyond its common focus on American and British archives" (18). By that measure, we still have some way to go.

NADINE ATTEWELL is associate professor in the Department of English and Cultural Studies at McMaster University.

JOHN R. GRAM

The Cherokee Diaspora: An Indigenous History of Migration, Resettlement, and Identity
by Gregory D. Smithers
Yale University Press, 2015

FOR MOST INDIGENOUS PEOPLES, it is difficult to imagine a group identity not inherently connected to a particular homeland, usually given as a sacred trust by a spiritual benefactor. What happens to Indigenous group identity and cohesion, then, when the homeland is lost? In his new book, Gregory D. Smithers convincingly demonstrates that not only did Cherokee identity survive a series of migrations and resettlements—voluntary and involuntary—between the Seven Years' War and World War II, but that the Cherokee actively engaged these very forces in crafting a sense of who they were as a people in response to the pressures of American settler-colonialism.

In the decades leading up to the forced removals of the 1830s, the Cherokee world came under increasing pressure from the expanding American nation, particularly in the form of frontier violence. Starting in the late eighteenth century, some Cherokee decided that the best response to these pressures was to move westward into Texas, Arkansas, and Missouri. Even as they struggled to preserve traditional knowledge and traditional kinship ties with those they left behind, Cherokee in diaspora created new ways to understand what it meant to be and live as Cherokee—ways that relied increasingly less on living in physical proximity to "home." The traditional stories portrayed the Cherokee ancestors as a migratory people; thus, there was nothing incompatible between being Cherokee and living outside the cis-Mississippi homeland.

Meanwhile, those who remained in the Southeast faced their own challenges in preserving and crafting a sense of Cherokee identity. A growing body of mixed-blood elites gradually came to control the larger Cherokee response, considering the possibilities and risks of Western education, Christianity, race-based slavery, and American legal and political traditions. Smithers demonstrates, however, that mixed-blood elites sought to adopt American influences in a manner consistent with what they saw as the best of traditional Cherokee beliefs and practices, while bringing about critical changes necessary to prepare the Cherokee for the future. Certainly not all Cherokee agreed with the new identity that the mixed-blood elites were crafting, but among the elites themselves a rough consensus seems apparent. Despite this consensus, some elites concluded that not only could migration preserve Cherokee identity, but also that it was necessary for Cherokee survival. Eventually these elites would form the Treaty Party.

Following the forced removals of the 1830s, cis-Mississippi Cherokee found themselves reunited with the trans-Mississippi Cherokee of those earlier voluntary migrations. Not only did the Cherokee who endured forced removal now have to work out internal conflicts between Ross Party and Treaty Party forces, but they also had to learn how to coexist with those who had preceded them West. Again the Cherokee found themselves facing questions of identity, proper community organization and governance, and the importance and meaning of "home." Meanwhile the new Cherokee nation in Oklahoma also had to define what it meant to be "Cherokee" in light of those individuals and groups who still lived in diaspora yet claimed to be Cherokee—most notably the Cherokee living in North Carolina, who had managed to avoid removal.

Following the Civil War, the need to understand who was and was not Cherokee grew even more vital. Federal annuities were limited. The territory of the Cherokee nation had been greatly reduced, and both the land and the nation as a political entity came under threat from the Dawes and later Curtis Acts. Furthermore, decades of migration and intermarriage now meant that the Cherokee diaspora was potentially quite large now. Simple definitions of who was and was not "Cherokee" were not easy to come by. The last portion of the book describes how the Cherokee nation wrestled to create a legal definition of Cherokee citizenship. Smithers's discussion of how the notion of "blood" entered this discussion and its subsequent effect on Cherokee freedmen is particularly nuanced and effective.

By recontextualizing the forced removals of the 1830s within a much larger pattern of migration and resettlement between the Seven Years' War and World War II, Smithers does a tremendous service to both Cherokee historiography and historical memory. No future work will be able to ignore his interpretation. By demonstrating how the oft-separate fields of Indigenous, diaspora, and migration studies can benefit from being in conversation with one another, Smithers offers a fruitful roadmap that future scholars would be wise to utilize.

JOHN R. GRAM is an instructor in the History Department at Missouri State University.

MICHAEL LERMA

Neoliberal Indigenous Policy: Settler Colonialism and the "Post-Welfare"
   State
by Elizabeth Strakosch
Palgrave Macmillan, 2015

STRAKOSCH HAS BROUGHT TO LIGHT a veiled, contemporary, systematic attack on Indigenous sovereignty around the world. Indigenous nations remain under attack in a "liberal democracy"—dominated world. Typically, the genocidal four (also known as Australia, Canada, New Zealand, and the United States) are regarded as the vanguards of liberal democracy. A more accurate description might be to call them the defenders of white hetero-patriarchic democracy. Strakosch has effectively called into question the legitimacy of these nations to "incorporate" Indigenous populations into domestic institutions of marginalization.

Her argument is clear and convincing. Settler-colonial projects have practiced a liberal norm of marginalizing all but white males. These projects slowly incorporate nonwhite males over time. This is a centuries-long process. In the twenty-first century, these projects continue and, perhaps, are even more hostile to Indigenous rights. Rather than collaborate or cooperate with Indigenous sovereigns, as nations, settler states (or colonial actors) have opted to individualize Indigenous rights. This strategy works to delegitimize Indigenous sovereigns. With no clear defender of individual Indigenous rights, Indigenous citizens are usurped further into colonial domestic polities. Hence, Indigenous individuals are granted limited access to political and economic institutions. They will not get the best access but they will get to legitimately complain about it. Most complaints will be heard and dismissed.

Strakosch's work offers empirical evidence of exchanging Indigenous rights founded within precolonial settler sovereignty for domestic institutions founded in colonial settler states. The case study evidence is undeniable. Colonial actors have worked systematically to dismantle, piece by piece, Indigenous institutions of sovereignty. In sum, settler states may claim to have represented Indigenous populations. In reality, it appears Indigenous individuals have been further marginalized with no opportunity to return to a time when Indigenous sovereignty, at least, had to be tolerated.

One of the best contributions of Strakosch's work involves what I might call a "blame the victim" approach. The case of Australia's public policy reform seems packaged in seemingly "fair" language about shared responsibility. This assumption holds only if Indigenous peoples can be faulted for surviving genocide. (Blaming Indigenous peoples for their survival is a tried and true colonial tactic.) By framing contemporary neoliberal policy as something for which Indigenous individuals must take responsibility ignores the projects carried out by the genocidal four. I only wish Strakosch was more fierce in this position. The reality is that settler projects destroy Indigenous nations' ability to feed themselves in the course of war. They destroyed Indigenous political economies. When Indigenous peoples could no longer feed themselves, they could no longer defend their traditional homelands. Settler states, then, build their own economic institutions, based in liberalism, by monopolizing Indigenous natural resources. Claiming that Indigenous peoples must take responsibility for their own colonization takes amazing intestinal fortitude.

The theoretical contributions are a welcome commentary in opposition not only to settler-colonialism projects but also to an Indigenous elite that seems to happily cooperate. It seems that many Indigenous leaders should read this book in order to understand better their own culpability in serving colonial projects. Sadly, understanding neoliberal consequences is just a small step. In reality, settler states fund economic development tied to Indigenous peoples only when it furthers neoliberal goals of resource monopolization. Few Indigenous communities can meaningfully refuse settler money. This problem will continue to prevent meaningful economic development that is complementary to Indigenous worldviews.

It is heartening to see scholarship emerge questioning the very legitimacy of colonial actors as sovereigns. Why are settler states always assumed to be the correct containers for Indigenous rights? This assumption is especially problematic because liberalism itself seems incapable of assuming a collective, such as an Indigenous nation or community, and would rather default Indigenous individuals to a settler state citizen scenario. Strakosch has masterfully highlighted the immense negative consequences of domestic policy envelopment. What's more, many Indigenous citizens seem to be welcoming, or at least powerless to question, the adoption of Western legal frames to first establish and then defend Indigenous rights.

Overall this is a great book highlighting a sorely under-researched topic. My only criticism is that the work can go further by utilizing small-n research methodologies to demonstrate more concretely, and empirically, the systematic demise of Indigenous rights. My hope is that this work will cause contemporary Indigenous scholars to rethink their own policy positions.

MICHAEL LERMA (P'urhépecha) is associate professor of politics and international affairs and applied Indigenous studies at Northern Arizona University.

PAUL McKENZIE-JONES

Gathering the Potawatomi Nation: Revitalization and Identity
by Christopher Wetzel
University of Oklahoma Press, 2015

CHRISTOPHER WETZEL has produced a fascinating history of the successful rebuilding of the Potawatomi, from a disparate group of nine bands situated across four states and two countries, into a nation that stands as a modern conceptualization of true Indigenous self-determination. Beginning and ending with the annual Gathering of the Potawatomi Nation that encapsulates both the book's title and its core theme, the text has a circular rather than a linear structural framework that better suits the Indigenous nationalist worldview within its pages.

Within that structure, the book is divided into two parts, "Roots of the Nation" and "Routes to the Nation," which clearly delineate the fracturing of the nation that has necessitated the need to rebuild it. In the first part, Wetzel identifies two major events of Potawatomi history that facilitated the early schism in the cohesive unity that bound the various bands of Potawatomi peoples together. The first, the Treaty of Chicago in 1833, resulted in massive losses of land for the Potawatomi as well as a diaspora, the effects of which have taken several generations to repair. As bands scattered west, or fled to Canada to escape the unrelenting surge of white settlement, others tried to stay behind only to be subjected to the Trail of Death, the second major event, as hundreds of remaining Potawatomi were forced into Kansas.

In the second part of the book, Wetzel describes how the shared band memories, and shifting perceptions, of these events has enabled national brokers—culturally immersed band members (several of whom are profiled within the text), who reach across the many divides in what Wetzel describes as intra-national relationships, to renegotiate a national narrative of togetherness and community. Whereas for much of the twentieth century the different bands competed for just reparations from the land losses of the Treaty of Chicago and kept open the wounds of diaspora and localized differences, a later focus on the traumas of the Trail of Death reminded band members of their shared identities and histories. A common goal of language revitalization across the different bands also helped cement that communal unity of national identity.

And it is here that the annual Gathering of the Potawatomi Nation becomes more than just a communal festival of culture and takes on new meaning as a reinvigoration of nationhood that confounds competing federal colonial relationships of U.S. or Canadian oversight of the various bands and declares that the Potawatomi will be recognized as a single nation irrespective of which side of the settler-colonial border an individual band may reside. One other vitally important aspect of this contemporary rebuilding and re-articulation of the Potawatomi Nation has been the commitment to follow as many of the traditional forms of organization and representation as were followed in the days before fragmentation laid the old nation to rest. Wetzel assures the reader several times throughout the text that this new conceptualization of Potawatomi nationhood was not won at the expense of traditional relationships but because of them, again emphasizing the importance of the aforementioned national brokers.

One of the most impressive aspects of Wetzel's book is the sheer number of oral histories and personal perspectives of Potawatomi citizens from all bands he has included. Hearing from the people involved in the monumental effort of decades of networking and negotiating the different, often competing needs of youth, elders, reservation, and urban citizens gives us a human rather than structural view of Potawatomi nationhood. This is the real strength of the book, in that as well researched and meticulously chronicled as it is, Wetzel leaves the final word to Potawatomi citizens themselves. His concluding chapter on "Future Directions" of the Potawatomi Nation is a space he has reserved for personal responses on the revitalization and rejuvenation of shared nationhood from leaders of five of the nine Potawatomi bands.

In conclusion, Wetzel's text is an important part of the new historiography of Indigenous strength, unity, and revitalization that is shaping twenty-first-century Indigenous studies and taking hope from Indigenous peoples and communities, not just in North America but across the world. He highlights how the diligence of cultural and linguistic tenacity, and political ingenuity, together with the sheer stubborn will of people committed to their cause, can bring a nation back to life, as strong now as it was in the past, with hope and certainty of a vibrant future before it.

PAUL McKENZIE-JONES is assistant professor in Native American studies at Montana State University—Northern.

LIANNE MARIE LEDA CHARLIE

Free to Be Mohawk: Indigenous Education at the Akwesasne Freedom School
by Louellyn White
University of Oklahoma Press, 2015

WHAT DOES IT MEAN TO BE "FULLY MOHAWK"? In *Free to Be Mohawk: Indigenous Education at the Akwesasne Freedom School,* Mohawk scholar Louellyn White addresses this question through a detailed historiographical and contemporary account of the Akwesasne Freedom School (AFS), a small, community controlled Mohawk language school in the Akwesasne Mohawk community (also known as St. Regis, Quebec / New York State). The school was born out of political conflict that consumed the community in the late 1970s, which highlighted a desire from community members for a space where Mohawk youth could reclaim their culture and their identity. The result was AFS. Today it is an example of a self-sufficient, community-driven, independent education program that operates free of both U.S. and Canadian state funding and control. *Free to Be Mohawk* tells the story of the Akwesasne Nation's expression of their right to education sovereignty and shows how AFS was designed to counter and transcend colonialism through a culturally specific curriculum and Mohawk language immersion.

White carried out her research on AFS in direct response to a request from the AFS community, which wished for a research project that traced the impact of the school on the lives of its students and also documented the school's history. White has provided readers with a resource that does the latter, as well as situating AFS within a broader conversation that explores the links between self-determination and education. Her work also speaks to how Native scholars can go about doing research with and for their own communities, as well as to the power and potential of Indigenous, critical pedagogy in countering the legacy and contemporary effects of continued settler-colonialism.

White combines interviews with AFS students, teachers, and alumni; participant observation in the classroom at the school; and curriculum review and archival research to tell the story of AFS. A number of insights are revealed through White's research. Here I address three. One, the experience of students and teachers at AFS counter the oft-held belief that immersion or tribal schools are less academically rigorous than public schools. *Free to Be Mohawk* reveals that students at AFS not only performed well academically, they were strong in their identity and culture and had proficient Mohawk language capabilities. Two, the link between Indigenous language acquisition and identity formation is complex. *Free to Be Mohawk* reveals that language acquisition, while important, is not necessarily the basis of identity construction; in other words, being fluent in Mohawk does not equate to being "fully Mohawk." Other components are just as necessary and required for identity construction—song, dance, cultural teachings and practices, social connection, and so forth—all of which can be enhanced in educational settings that are rooted in cultural content and utilize holistic pedagogies. Finally, *Free to Be Mohawk* also reinforces the importance of language use at home, in addition to at the schools, as a way to support Indigenous language acquisition and revitalization.

Free to Be Mohawk is an important contribution to the field of Indigenous education and Indigenous language revitalization. It is useful to communities and scholars interested in language immersion, decolonial identity construction, and critical pedagogy, as well as the praxis of Indigenous self-determination and nationhood-building via educational initiatives. White's work is especially revealing about the realities of community-controlled education initiatives with respect to cost, time, commitment, and levels of community/parental involvement. Her work also speaks to the level of freedom available to schools that operate outside state control with respect to curriculum development, organization structure, teacher training, and policies.

White's work is a valuable contribution to the growing body of research on Indigenous communities that are exercising their inherent right to education sovereignty. As a young Indigenous educator, I am curious about the ways that communities are developing their own culturally relevant curriculum, and the creative and culturally informed ways they are teaching it. Perhaps future work in this area might include more examples of actual curriculum, either as ethnographic illustrations of practices within the classroom or appendices that include descriptions of curriculum and detailed best practices. In my experience, it seems that communities are often starting from scratch when developing their own curriculum, especially language revitalization curriculum. Such additions might make work like White's even more useful to other communities and educators engaged in or beginning their own education sovereignty initiatives.

LIANNE MARIE LEDA CHARLIE (Tagé Cho Hudän) is a PhD student in the Indigenous Politics Program at the University of Hawai'i at Mānoa.

JOSHUA L. REID

Rivers, Fish, and the People: Tradition, Science, and Historical Ecology
  of Fisheries in the American West
edited by Pei-Lin Yu
University of Utah Press, 2015

MUCH OF THE RICHNESS in Native American and Indigenous studies comes from the interdisciplinary approaches we take in our scholarship and through diverse collaborations with Indigenous communities. In a similar vein, *Rivers, Fish, and the People* strives to reflect recent collaborations between researchers and Native peoples. Combining ethnographic information, historical ecology, and archaeology, the contributors detail the environmental and cultural contexts of several rivers in the North American West to determine what was being harvested, and how, in the past before the historical period.

In their examination of rivers and fisheries from northern California to southern British Columbia and east to the Columbia Plateau, the contributors demonstrate the ways that Indigenous fishers "coped with significant variability in access to fish" (191). For example, geologic and other natural events along the Snake River periodically disrupted salmon runs, as Mark Plew and Stacey Guinn argue. This meant that communities along the Middle Snake River relied more on foraging than fishing for long periods of time. This conclusion echoes the work of Anna Marie Prentiss, another contributor to this volume, who has argued that the decline in salmon runs along the Fraser River during the early Medieval Warm Period (around 750–1250 CE) encouraged an expansion in diet breadth among St'át'imc villages. In his chapter on secondary resources along the Lower Spokane River, Jason Jones finds that Indigenous populations relied on collecting freshwater shellfish "to counter unplanned resource deficits" (148). This strategy was not simply one of shifting to any other resource during poor salmon runs; instead, it was a planned harvest of a reliably available food that exemplified successful resource intensification to offset salmon run fluctuations. Similarly, Kevin Lyons reveals that in the absence of salmon, Kalispels fished extensively for other species and in many of the same ways as they did for salmon. Together, these contributors reveal that even among the "Salmon People," customary subsistence was more complex and diverse than previously assumed.

The chapters also illustrate that Indigenous fishers of the North American West were not passive consumers—many engaged in practices that enhanced the productivity of some fisheries. For instance, Plains Miwoks of northern California used fire and other management strategies to "optimize habitat conditions" for fish in their efforts to "adapt to fluctuating environmental conditions" in the Lower Cosumnes River watershed (180). As Michelle Stevens and Emilie Zelazo find, controlled burns helped manage the landscape to maximize the availability of natural materials used for fishing nets and to keep the floodplain clean and clear for juvenile fish. In an intriguing chapter, Pei-Lin Yu and Jackie Cook combine ethnographic evidence and new research in lithic tools to demonstrate a "large-scale but flexible and adaptive, system of anadromous fish procurement and processing" at a Kettle Falls site on the Columbia River (90). Yu and Cook detail the staggering amount of labor to process salmon, estimating that women spent approximately a third of each year engaged in and preparing for this activity.

Despite many of the chapters' specific strengths and the editor's claims about what the volume accomplishes, it falls short in engaging more fully with Indigenous methodologies. For instance, Stephen Grabowski's chapter about the biology and ecology of Pacific salmon missed the opportunity to draw from Indigenous knowledges of fish and waterways. When considering how some archaeologists use the dearth of fishing equipment and fish bone remains to infer that the ethnographic record overstates the importance of salmon, Yu and Cook helpfully remind the reader that archaeology does not happen in a vacuum—these studies "have real social, political, and legal consequences for Native American communities today" (73). Ignoring this key tenet of Indigenous methodology, Plew and Guinn's otherwise excellent chapter makes this inference along these lines. Similarly, many of the contributors neglect to decolonize the very nature of archaeology or ecology, assuming that these scientific approaches act as an "objective grounding [that] provides needful sideboards in the reading of ethnohistoric data" (108). This volume could have been an especially useful intervention if the contributors had followed the lead of historical archaeologists in applying Indigenous methodologies. While leaving plenty of room for subsequent scholars to forge new ground in combining ethnohistoric information and science, though, *Rivers, Fish, and the People* provides a useful collection of case studies illustrating the various adaptive relationships that Indigenous peoples in the North American West crafted with rivers and fish.

JOSHUA L. REID (Snohomish) is associate professor in history and American Indian studies at the University of Washington.

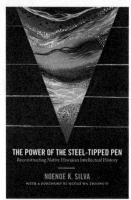

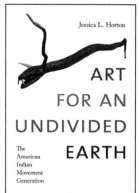

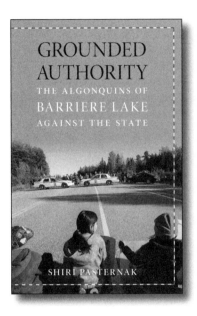
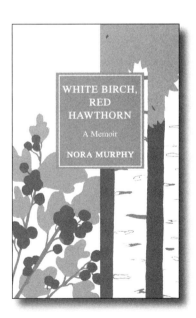

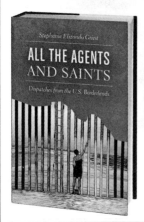
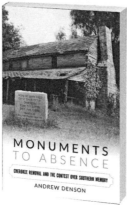

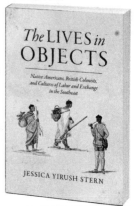